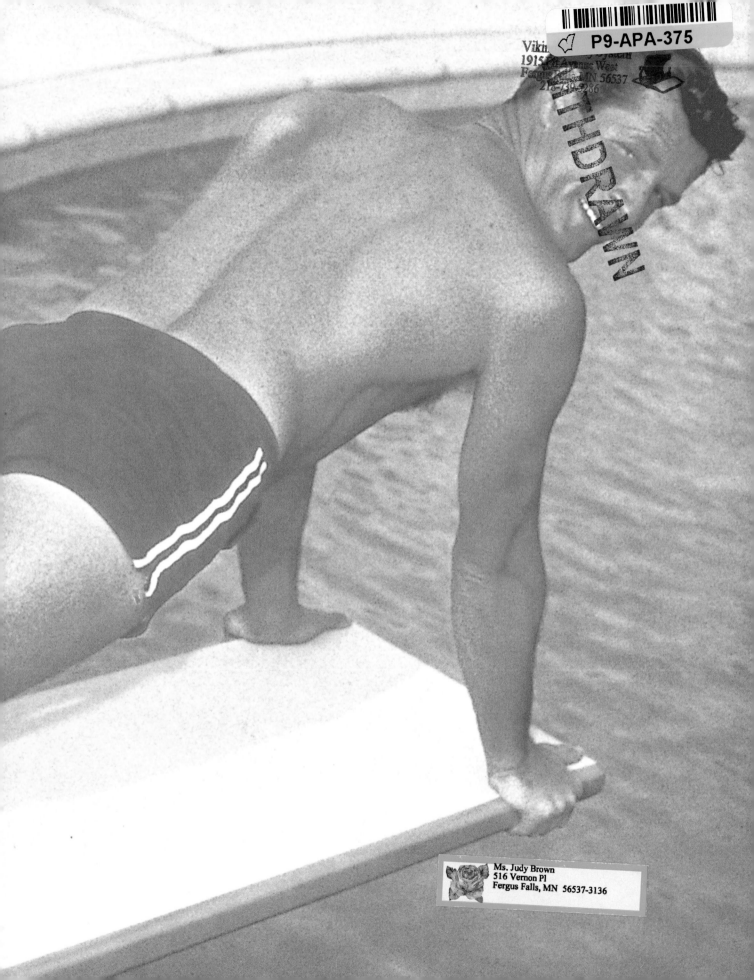

heartthrob

donald f. reuter

UNIVERSE PUBLISHING

creative direction and design by Donald F. Reuter for **alias** BOOKS

First published in the
United States
by UNIVERSE PUBLISHING
A Division of Rizzoli
International Publications, Inc.
300 Park Avenue South
New York, NY 10010

©1998 Donald F. Reuter and

alias
BOOKS

98 99 00 / 10 9 8 7 6 5 4 3 2 1

ISBN: 0-7893-0224-1

Printed in Singapore

Library of Congress Catalog
Card Number: 98-61103

Front cover
Guy Madison *(Photofest)*

Back cover
Jeffrey Hunter *(Kobal)*

This book is dedicated to all the "heartthrobs" in the world—past, present, *and* future. And to any and all who have known the indescribable pleasure of being in their company.

opening page
Harry Belafonte (b. 1929)
Gorgeous, husky-voiced singer, whose fame came during the mid-'50s "calypso-craze" with his number-one hit, "Banana Boat (Day-O)." Often considered music's first black male sex symbol, he acted sporadically in films. Among them, *Carmen Jones* (1954) and *Islands in the Sun* (1957). Tony Award winner for *John Murray Anderson's Almanac* in 1957, and Grammy Award winner. (*The Everett Collection*)

previous page
Robert Wagner (b. 1930)
Spotted by talent scout Henry Wilson, while still at college, Wagner began his career as 20th Century Fox's "pretty boy" lead of the early 1950s. By decade's end, his roles took on more maturity (even a touch of malice). Later became an even greater success on television: "It Takes a Thief" (1968-71), "Switch" (1975-78), and "Hart to Hart" (1978-83). Twice married to actress Natalie Wood (until her death in 1981). Now wed to actress Jill St. John. (*Corbis-Bettmann*)

left
Dan O'Brien (b. 1966)
In a sport notorious for turning out "studs" (Bob Mathias, Rafer Johnson, and Bruce Jenner, among them), Dan is the pefect '90s version of the decathlete. Born of a mixed ethnic background (his mother is Finnish and father is African American), he's a disarming visual blend of the two. Add to that a body to die for, a great personality, and this Olympic gold-medal winner (in 1996) is a champion by any standards. Has a smile that'll knock your socks off. (*David Klutho/Sports Illustrated*)

Contributors

The author would like to give extra special thanks to the following group of individuals who gave so generously of their time. The work would not be nearly as insightful or interesting without their thoughts and comments.

tyson beckford · geoffrey beene

naomi Campbell · Cindy Crawford

douglas fairbanks, jr. · amy fine Collins

eileen ford · nancy friday

Olivia goldsmith · farley granger

helen gurley brown · thomas hoving

tab hunter · donna karan

Michael lafavore · greg louganis

isaac Mizrahi · jim Moore

herb ritts · isabella rossellini

Claudia Schiffer · Michelangelo Signorile

ingrid Sischy · Mark Spitz

gloria Steinem · Susan toepfer

linda Wells

right
Robert Stack (b. 1919)
Slightly cold version of "the-boy-next-door," Stack's career was launched as "the first boy to kiss Deanna Durbin" in the film, *First Love* (1939). Lucky girl! Went on to similar roles before serving in the navy in WW II. Upon returning, starred in *The High and the Mighty* (1954) and his Oscar-nominated role (as supporting actor) in *Written on the Wind* (1957). Greatest success: his Emmy-winning role as Eliot Ness, in "The Untouchables" (1956-63). Best-kept secret: his absolutely superb body. Easily one of the best pre-Schwarzenegger physiques in Hollywood. (*Kobal*)

following page
Barry Coe (b. 1934)
Meteoric rising and swiftly falling teen idol of the late '50s, whose best-remembered work may be as Rodney in "Peyton Place" (1957). Went on to do a short-lived TV series, "Follow the Sun," in 1961, and a stint on the daytime soap, "General Hospital." (*MacFadden/Corbis-Bettmann*)

"The one trend in film that never stops is the need for beauty."
– Farley Granger

table of Contents

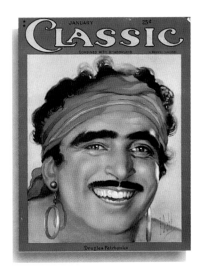

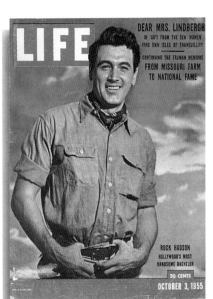

First of all, let me say that I do not consider myself an *expert* on the subject of male beauty. I believe I am more an *enthusiast*, as it was once so eloquently put to me. (Besides, that sounds so much more like the experience of putting a book together like this, than *expert*, which has far too clinical a connotation for such a sexy subject.) Furthermore, since beauty is supposed to be "in the eye of the beholder," then we could all be considered experts and make our own versions of this book (which on some level, I expect, is precisely what you will do after perusing through its pages). This then brings me to why I thought this book was a good idea. I knew there would be a slew of publications celebrating some aspect or other of the 20th century, and indeed there are—from the "most entertaining people" to the "most influential" of the entire one hundred years and everything in between. But not one devoted entirely to the celebration of good-looking men. And why not? Possibly because in most situations men (and their admirers) don't like to *openly* admit to the attraction. Well, let me tell you (as if you didn't already know) from the beginning of time, handsome "hunky" men have ruled the Earth, maybe even to a degree that outstrips their female counterparts. The 20th century in particular, with all its glorious pop culture excessiveness, has given us a bumper crop of beautiful boys. If that's not reason enough, I don't know what is. But more importantly, I felt that behind every picture of a good-looking man is an underlying cultural, sociological, and political reason that helped to create it. If you don't believe me, just think about it for a moment. For every Antonio Sabato, Jr. underwear ad, there had to be a Burt Reynolds centerfold. For every sullen Brad Pitt portrait, a Montgomery Clift had to hesitantly pose for his. I think you get the picture.

I also wanted to do a book on the subject (of male beauty) because of my own personal experiences. The question of what makes someone (male or female) attractive has always held particular interest. You see, whether I liked it or not, I grew up in a social environment that seemed to presage my fascination with the topic. My mother was Korean and my father was German-American. Physically, they both bore the hallmarks of their individual ethnicities (quite beautifully, I might add); Mom was petite, olive-skinned, almond-eyed, and had black-lacquered hair. Dad was tall, muscular, blond, and blue-eyed. As you can imagine, my sister, brother, and I ended up with a mixed bag of the two. Though I can't speak for either one of my siblings in this regard, I know that in my case, the resulting physical combination was potent. I was the classic "half-breed," to borrow a title from the Cher song. Growing up and going through school was especially arduous; I looked decidedly Asian (at that time), but felt completely Anglo. Add the name-calling, from "chink" to "jap" (which always sounded a bit humorous considering I was neither one of those races) and the absence of any other children in similar circumstances and I was a mental mess. However, as I got older, the Germanic side started to kick in, slightly (though I never got the blond hair and blue eyes I wanted). By the time I moved to New York, still predisposed to slurs and derision,

introduction

I did not anticipate the general lack of "racial" recognition. People thought I was Slavik, Puerto Rican, Russian, you name it—they even began to see some of the German. Whatever it was, in the Big Apple I was happenin'. It seemed everybody who used to avoid me wanted to be my friend. Suddenly my Eurasian (I love that word) parentage created within me a valued commodity—I was exotic! Still, I never knew at any given moment why someone was attracted to or away from me, so often were the signals that unclear. No wonder I am obsessed with the way people look.

Heartthrob contains over two hundred and twenty pictures of different men (including only a handful who were lucky enough to appear twice). I did my best to include as well-rounded a group as possible, given the circumstances—most notably, space and budget. I started out with a list of over five hundred names (and, let me tell you, there were some real "honeys" on that list); but in order to keep that many in a book it would have had to be either twice as big (and expensive) or the pictures would have needed to run the size of postage stamps (and nobody liked that as an option). So, unfortunately, the initial group had to be narrowed down. And I knew, from the very beginning, there was little chance the choices would *not* be influenced by my own personal tastes and biases. How could it be any other way? Still, I made the effort to keep a lot in (that I did not necessarily like) and take a lot out (that I did). Early on, I also made the decisions not to focus (somewhat) on photographs of the most current "faves" (my feeling was, you could see a better picture of them in a magazine) and I went light on including television stars (mainly because they should have their own edition). In the process of finalizing the group, I confirmed these universal truths: that you cannot please everybody; your first choice is usually the best; and your mom and sister, present or not, consciously or unconsciously, will influence who you pick (Charlton Heston and Donny Osmond are just two of the fine-looking men who have them to thank for being pointedly included). Additionally, while it was not possible to accurately date each image, they were chosen to show the individual at his "prime." As arbitrary as that may sound, it was done with a deliberate understanding of what course their lives followed and how it affected and changed the way they looked.

Last, a little insight into the structure of *Heartthrob*. The pictures are divided into different categories, from "Dream Date" to "Boy-Next-Door," but don't let the labels fool you. The idea was to place the guy where he *seemed* most comfortable, knowing all along it would probably cause some consternation, because most of these gentlemen fit into more than one area (if any, really, at all). The comments from my learned contributors are also meant to illicit some meaningful dialogue among you readers. As they say, "a picture is worth a thousand words." Enjoy!

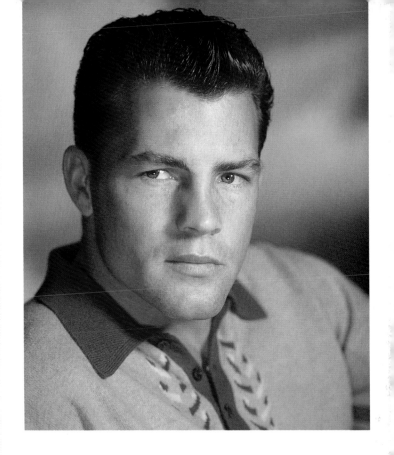

this page, top
Frank Gifford (b. 1930)
This handsome "superjock" is a College and Pro Football Hall-of-Famer, with an NFL career that lasted twelve years. One of the first pro-ballers to attract as much attention for his "BMOC" (Big Man on Campus) good looks as his adeptness on the playing field (four-time All-Pro, 1956 MVP), Gifford left the sport (namely, the New York Giants) to become an announcer, no doubt garnering the attention of many new female (and male) viewers across the country. (*Kobal*)

middle
Hugh O'Brian (b. 1925)
Tall, supermasculine "hunk" of a man, who, despite film appearances, is most notable as the TV title character in "The Life and Times of Wyatt Earp" (1955-61). (Author's collection)
Check out the book's endpapers for a great overall view of Hugh in the flesh. (*Kobal*)

(Author's note: As a byproduct of the times, many stars [male and female] were often called upon, or rather considered it an obligation, to investigate other areas of creative endeavor [for financial gain]. Most often it would lead to things like product endorsement, or, on occasion [whether the talent warranted it or not], things like a studio album. Most, as you can imagine were not great successes. But they do make charming conversation pieces!)

left
John Payne (1912–89)
Very likable, slickly handsome lead in, of all things, musicals and westerns, among other types of film. Some of his best work: *Hello Frisco, Hello* (1943) and as the-neighbor-across-the-hall in *Miracle on 34th Street* (1947). Best physical feature (at least in this photo): those massive thighs, so ably lit by master lensman George Hurrell. (*Baby Jane of Hollywood*)

right
Dennis Hopper (b. 1936)
Actor, director, and obviously, one-time "pretty boy." Despite good, though often small, roles in important films (*Giant* and *Rebel Without a Cause*), Hopper was considered difficult to work with, and, as his rebellious nature grew, found it harder and harder to find work. However, likely because of his spirited nature, he went on to coproduce the 1969 youth-classic *Easy Rider* (with Peter Fonda) to enormous worldwide success. During the '80s, many of his on-screen appearances took on a maniacal, somewhat psychotic edge, truly coming full circle from such a "pretty" start. Oscar nominee for *Hoosiers* (1986). (*MacFadden/Corbis-Bettmann*)

heartthrob

"Not so long ago, it would have been ludicrous to many people to consider the word 'beauty' with men. Today we know it is not inappropriate at all and realize, too, that the issues it still raises help us to understand who we are as individuals and where we are as a people."
— Ingrid Sischy

Matinee Idol

left
Richard Arlen
(1889–1976, Cornelius Richard Van Mattimore) Beefy, ebullient hero-star of silent and talkie films. Possibly his best-known film was the first Best Picture Oscar-winner, *Wings* (1927), where he played the friend of "pretty boy" Buddy Rogers. (*Everett Collection*)

right, top
Wallace Reid (1891–1923)
Boyishly handsome star (and often director) of dozens of silent films, whose career came to a tragic, early end. Debuting in film in 1910, by the late teens he was Paramount's top male star. But an accident (1919) en route to a location shooting resulted in a head injury, where doctors prescribed morphine to ease the pain. He continued working for many years, but became addicted to the drug, making it increasingly hard to focus on work. Placed in a sanitarium, he died in agony at thirty-two years of age. Once slated to star in the original version of *Ben-Hur* (1926), his role went to Ramon Novarro. (*Kobal*)

right, middle
Ramon Novarro (1899–1968)
Stunning, "Latin lover," who, along with Valentino and John Gilbert, ruled the romantic roost of Hollywood's Silent Era. His best role, however, was as the heroic title character in *Ben-Hur* (1926). Despite attempts for continued stardom in "talkies," his career waned. Sadly too, Novarro, who was widely considered gay, was found brutally murdered, at the hands of male hustlers, in his Hollywood home. (*MPTV Archives*)

right, bottom
Rudolph Valentino (1895–1926)
Perhaps the most famous screen lover of all time and certainly the first to receive legendary status in death. Unquestionably popular with female fans of the time, men found him too effeminate and quite dislikable, causing one critic to call him a "painted pansy." After watching *Monsieur Beaucaire* (1924) and *The Sheik* (1921), you can be your own judge. (*MPTV Archives*)

It all started with him, the "matinee idol." From the moment he appeared, our lives would never be the same. The man singlehandedly changed our visual landscape. And for the price of a movie ticket, we gladly doted on his every move, bought the cars he drove, wore the clothes he favored, and secretly yearned for his attention and affection. For the first time in history, adoration on this massive a scale was possible. (Thank you, Mr. Edison!) Before, maybe thousands would turn out to hear an opera star sing or watch a Shakespearean actor emote, but now millions of women (and men) together could worship

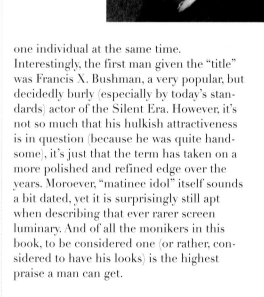

one individual at the same time. Interestingly, the first man given the "title" was Francis X. Bushman, a very popular, but decidedly burly (especially by today's standards) actor of the Silent Era. However, it's not so much that his hulkish attractiveness is in question (because he was quite handsome), it's just that the term has taken on a more polished and refined edge over the years. Moroever, "matinee idol" itself sounds a bit dated, yet it is surprisingly still apt when describing that ever rarer screen luminary. And of all the monikers in this book, to be considered one (or rather, considered to have his looks) is the highest praise a man can get.

"Even though we have idols (and beauty standards) today, we cannot presume there won't be another form of entertainment (possibly computer-generated) that will demand something else, making them obsolete."
— *Susan Toepfer*

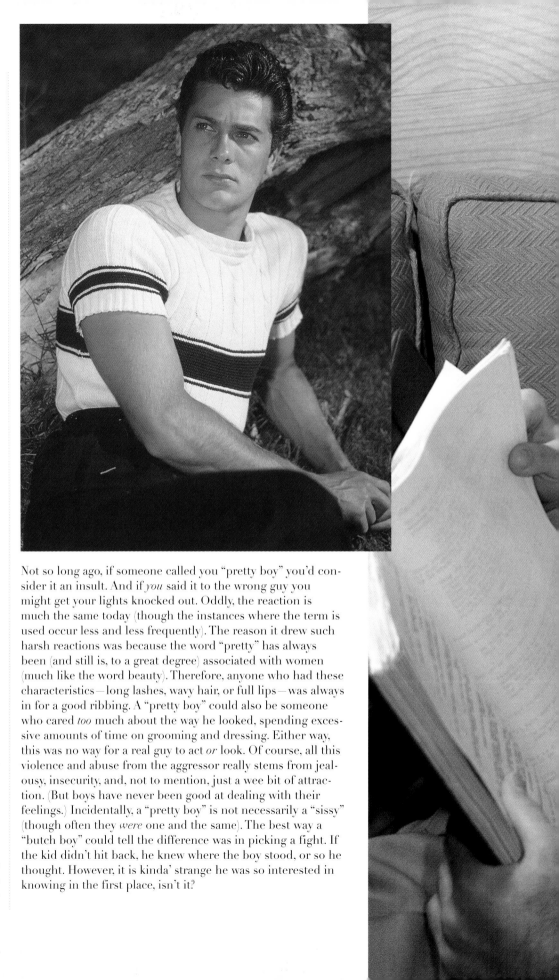

"Many men are so worried about the way they are perceived, that I've known male models who felt they had to carry a philosophy or law book with them to a shoot to be taken seriously (and considered masculine)."
--Cindy Crawford

Not so long ago, if someone called you "pretty boy" you'd consider it an insult. And if *you* said it to the wrong guy you might get your lights knocked out. Oddly, the reaction is much the same today (though the instances where the term is used occur less and less frequently). The reason it drew such harsh reactions was because the word "pretty" has always been (and still is, to a great degree) associated with women (much like the word beauty). Therefore, anyone who had these characteristics—long lashes, wavy hair, or full lips—was always in for a good ribbing. A "pretty boy" could also be someone who cared *too* much about the way he looked, spending excessive amounts of time on grooming and dressing. Either way, this was no way for a real guy to act *or* look. Of course, all this violence and abuse from the aggressor really stems from jealousy, insecurity, and, not to mention, just a wee bit of attraction. (But boys have never been good at dealing with their feelings.) Incidentally, a "pretty boy" is not necessarily a "sissy" (though often they *were* one and the same). The best way a "butch boy" could tell the difference was in picking a fight. If the kid didn't hit back, he knew where the boy stood, or so he thought. However, it is kinda' strange he was so interested in knowing in the first place, isn't it?

pretty boy

The "beau" is your one *special* guy. The one to go steady with—the perfect date. He's the fellow everyone's mom would like to see escorting you to a dance, with a corsage for you, looking natty in his white tuxedo with a red carnation. This is the boy both your parents would love to see you married to, because with him you'll be safe, happy, and secure. But you already knew all that—he's always been the perfect gentleman—never taking advantage of your affection, never trying anything untoward, always treating. Why couldn't all the other boys be like this?

left
Farley Granger (b. 1925)
Sighted at the age of seventeen, while still in high school, and cast as a Russian youth in his first film (for Samuel Goldwyn), 1943's *North Star.* Going off to war himself, he returned to play in such fantastic pseudo-sexual thrillers as *Rope* (1948) and *Strangers on a Train* (1951), both for Alfred Hitchcock, as well as Visconti's *Senso* (1954). Unhappy with the "pretty-boy-with-an-edge" roles he was being offered, Granger soon turned to stage and television. (*MacFadden/Corbis-Bettmann*)

right
Leonardo DiCaprio (b. 1974)
A Best Supporting Actor nominee for *What's Eating Gilbert Grape* (1993), beauteous and still-quite-boyish DiCaprio was on his way to becoming a very fine and accomplished actor. But that was well before his appearance in the monstrous hit *Titanic* (1997), making dear Leo into the dream-amour of countless teenage girls around the globe. For this alone, though, DiCaprio proved that a young female-skewed audience could turn a possibly disastrous film into a hit, and a relatively unknown, yet talented thespian, into a world-wide superstar. (*Piers MacDonald/Corbis*)

"I was only seventeen and on the cover of Look *magazine in 1942, and I had just filmed my first movie, North Star. All the attention was flattering in the beginning, then it just started to get old. Furthermore, the studio kept wanting me to play the same roles, but that gets wearing on the public and the individual. If you want to be a movie star, you figure, what the hell! I wanted to be an actor, not a type, so I escaped to the theatre. There they were not nearly as interested in what you looked liked, but whether or not you had talent."*
-- *Farley Granger*

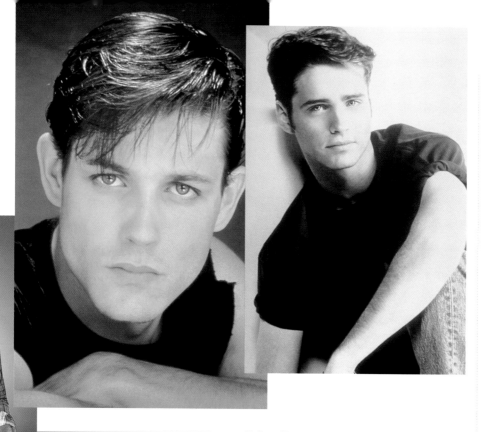

clockwise, from bottom left

Dan Cortese (b. 1967)
This '90s "super-beefcake" has had trouble
finding a vehicle worthy of his awesome body
and nearly too handsome face, although
recent success on "Veronica's Closet" (1997–)
may be just the place where he hangs his hat.
(*Everett Collection*)

Ted McGinley (b. 1958)
This ultra-handsome, surfer-blond type can be
seen adorning the pages of many early-'80s
fashion magazines, as a top male model of the
time. Invariably, his good looks would lead to
acting, and he signed on to play Marion Ross's
nephew on "Happy Days" (from 1980-84),
filling the void left by a departing Ron
Howard. He has also played roles on
"Dynasty," "Love Boat" and "Married...with
Children" (as next-door-neighbor Marcy's
husband, Jeff D'Arcy). (*Everett Collection*)

Gary Sandy (b. 1945)
The epitome of '70s "boy toy," who, in his first
prime-time series, Norman Lear's "All That
Glitters" (1977), was said to have the "best lit-
tle buns" in his company. Subsequent viewers
of his always tightly jean-clad posterior (as
Andy Travis) in the hit show "WKRP in
Cincinnati" (1978-82) would have to agree.
(*Everett Collection*)

Michael Pare (b. 1959)
Onetime chef and model, Pare started acting
(on TV) in the show "Greatest American
Hero" (1981-82), but found his "greatest"
success as an actor and singer in the feature
film *Eddie and the Cruisers* (1983). (*Everett
Collection*)

Jason Priestley (b. 1969)
"Boy toys" reached their apex with the debut
of Aaron Spelling's TV-drama "Beverly Hills
90210" (1990–). However, from the beginning, "stud-muffin" Priestley would have to
share the teenthrob spotlight with Luke Perry,
Ian Ziering, and Brian Austin Green. (*Everett
Collection*)

right

John-Eric Hexum (1957–84)
With his telefilm appearance in 1983's "The
Making of a Male Model," this sapphire-blue-
eyed stunner forever became the "boy toy of
the ages." Simultaneously, his tragic death the
following year (from an accidental, self-inflict-
ed gunshot), cemented his cult standing
among "heartthrob" aficionados. (*Everett
Collection*)

Culturally speaking, the "boy toy" is one of
this century's most telling inventions.
Even though men (on some level) have
always been appreciated for the way they
looked, were it not for the sexual revolutions
of the late '60s (figuring in both the
women's and gay movements), would they
finally, and so outwardly,
be referred to in such *objectifying* terms.
Starting in the '70s, by the "Madonna Era"
of the '80s, the assimilation of this male
"plaything" into society would nearly be
complete.

*"I think we are all try-
ing to reach a goal of
'wholeness,' and
progress is often in a
direction we haven't
been. So, for women it
may lie in caring less
about our external
appearance, for men it
may lie in caring more."*
--Gloria Steinem

boy toy

Remember the game that all the girls (including many of us boys, especially if you had a sister) used to play called Mystery Date*? You know, the one with the nifty white plastic door in the center that would uncover your "escort" for the evening. And, depending on how you turned the knob (*and there was a trick to it*), you'd wind up with any one of a number of guys, ranging from the rather studious to jockish, and memorably, the horrifying "dud." (Although, honestly, he wasn't really that bad-looking, just in dire need of a comb.) Of course the prize catch was, to put it in the form of their famous ditty, ". . . he might be a dud, or he might be a . . . dream. Oooh, aaah." Well that's who the "dream date" is, handsome as the day is long and dressed to the nines. But keep in mind the important word here is "dream," so no matter how wonderful a time you might have in his resplendent company, he can never be all yours. So even though this is the guy you *think* you want waiting behind your own nifty white plastic door, ready to carry you off in a splendid black convertible, to an evening filled with festivity, frivolity and "falling in love," in reality you're more likely to find happiness with someone simpler, more fallible, like the "boy-next-door." But even apart from that, expecting this devastating fantasy Prince Charming to turn up on your doorstep is only likely to happen if you live in the colored-cardboard world of childhood games.

right

Tab Hunter (b. 1931, Arthur Galien)
Perhaps no individual personifies "heartthrob" better than Tab Hunter. Appearing just as the studio system was winding down, Tab's superb good looks and athletic visage were a publicist's dream, and his emergence coincided nicely with that of an enormous (and growing) teen market. However, the propagation of his image eclipsed much of the true essence of the gentleman himself and his work was harshly judged by critics. Nevertheless, Hunter was idolized by millions and became a "poster boy" of the '50s. Among some of his better (often underrated) works are: *Battle Cry* (1955), *Damn Yankees* (1958), and the wonderfully self-effacing cult classic *Polyester* (1981) for director John Waters. Incidentally, Hunter was also an accomplished singer, responsible for the supersmash '50s teen-romance anthem, "Young Love." Best look: if he's your type, impossible to choose. (*MacFadden/Corbis-Bettmann*)

"I've always been uncomfortable with too many people around. Basically, I'm a very private person. But in Hollywood, getting attention is the name of the game. They are going to market you just like a product in a grocery store, hoping the public will want to take you off the shelf. It becomes a double-edged sword; you want to succeed and grow as an individual, but the labels, like 'heartthrob,' and the publicity, don't always allow you to be who you really are."
-- *Tab Hunter*

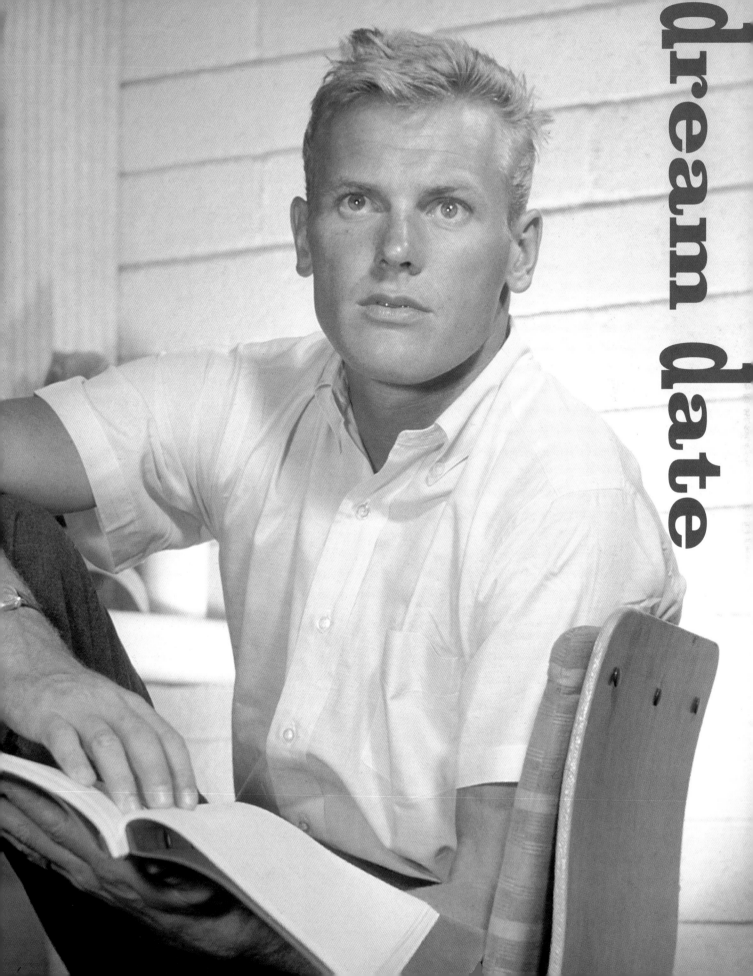

dream date

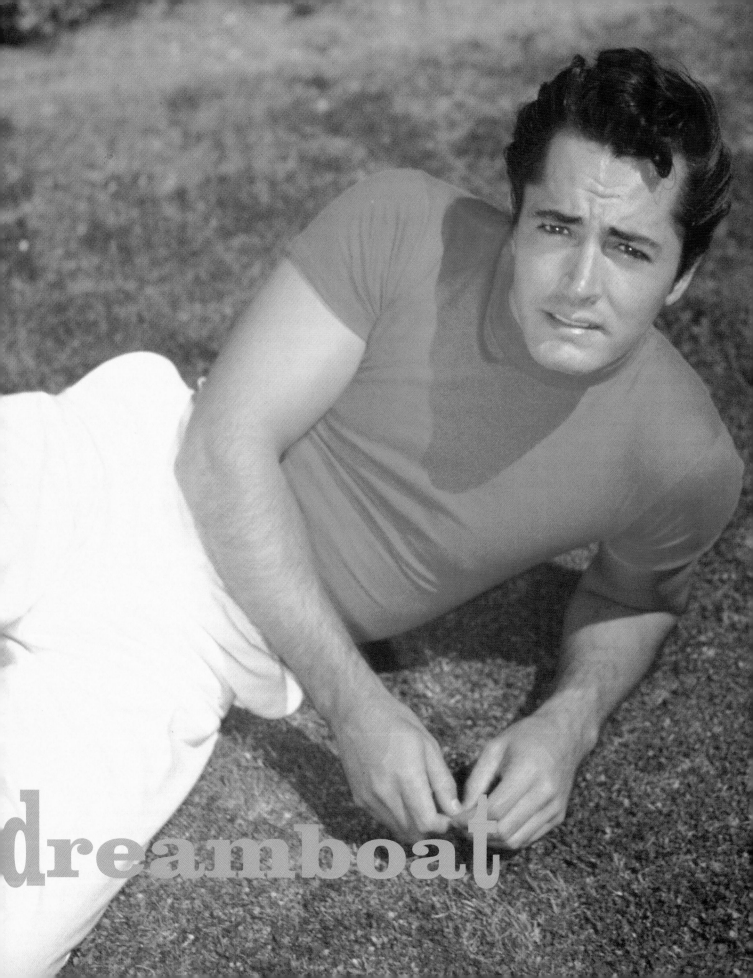

dreamboat

"Dreamboat" has a sweetly figurative meaning behind it. It refers to someone so indescribably beautiful that to be in his company is like being placed softly on board an open vessel, and set to float and drift through the clouds and currents of your barely conscious mind. Only to come back down from your rapt reverie at the sound of his voice, calling your name.

far left
John Derek (1926–98)
Well-known today for his marriages to Ursula Andress, Linda Evans, and Bo (Derek), John, when he first started out in Hollywood, was easily as "pretty" as any of his beautiful wives. Though, for all of his good looks and great build (and it was great), he did not find happiness in his own film career (mainly consisting of films geared to a young female audience) and took to photography, most famously ending as the film *auteur* of his last wife's career. Look for his oiled pecs in *The Ten Commandments* (1956). (*Kobal*)

near left, top
Paul Newman (b. 1925)
This "blue-eyed wonder" seems by many accounts to be the "heartthrob-of-the-century." Acting since the early '50s, Newman manages a career that would be the envy of any actor (despite the occasional misstep). One-time Oscar winner (for 1986's *The Color of Money*), this twice-married (most notably to actress Joanne Woodward since 1958), salad-dressing-making, auto-racing superstar has, in his own words, never considered himself a "sex symbol." (*MacFadden/Corbis-Bettmann*)

near left, bottom
Warren Beatty (b. 1937)
Super-pretty-sometimes-bad-boy sibling of actress Shirley MacLaine, Beatty shot to stardom in the early '60s, with such great flicks as *Splendor in the Grass* and *The Roman Spring of Mrs. Stone* (both 1961). Accomplished both in front of and behind the camera (as Oscar-winning director of 1981's *Reds*), Warren's real-life romantic shenanigans (Joan Collins, Leslie Caron, Madonna, et. al.) have been as instrumental to his rise to fame as his talent, though of late he has finally settled down with actress Annette Bening. (*MacFadden Corbis-Bettmann*)

"There is a conflict with what men want—to look good and be attractive to women and other men—and how they deal with it. They sort of blunder around, treating it like a secret, because most men wouldn't be caught dead admitting they thought about it."
—Michael Lafavore

If all the information you received about the pending visit from an unknown suitor was, "tall, dark, and handsome," wouldn't you breathe a sigh of relief? Well, to much of the world it seems, no three words better conjure up the ultimate (female to male) physical ideal than this trio of adjectives, and upon hearing them, we can all collectively exhale. Surely other attempts were made to string such wholly subjective words together, though it is likely that the results—like "tall, medium, and handsome"—did not have quite the same effect on listeners. Frustrated, too, must be the male who qualifies on only two levels; for true grace can be given only to those men who successfully embrace all three. (Besides, which duo would you pick?) And, in a world where being a blond was supposed to mean you had more "fun," isn't it interesting how the absence of these "fair-haired" brothers (therein) speaks volumes on what *some* women feel about "light-topped" members of our sex reaching that masculine pinnacle.

"Some individuals will have the 'star-quality' they're looking for, some won't, and it should be left at that. It's when someone tries to manufacture 'it' that things go wrong—it's all studied and attitude with no depth. It's more interesting and special when it occurs naturally."
— *Tab Hunter*

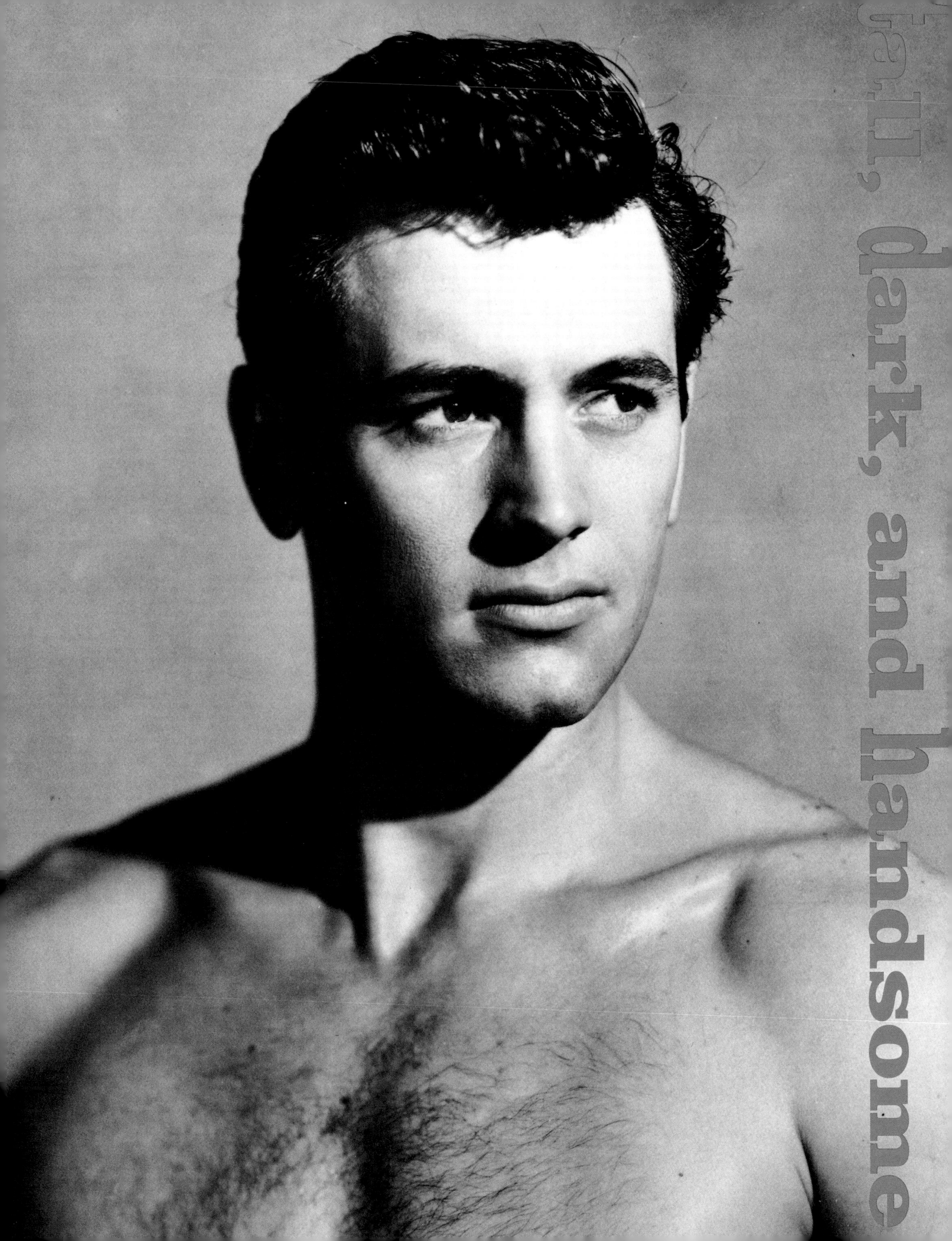
ll, dark, and handsome

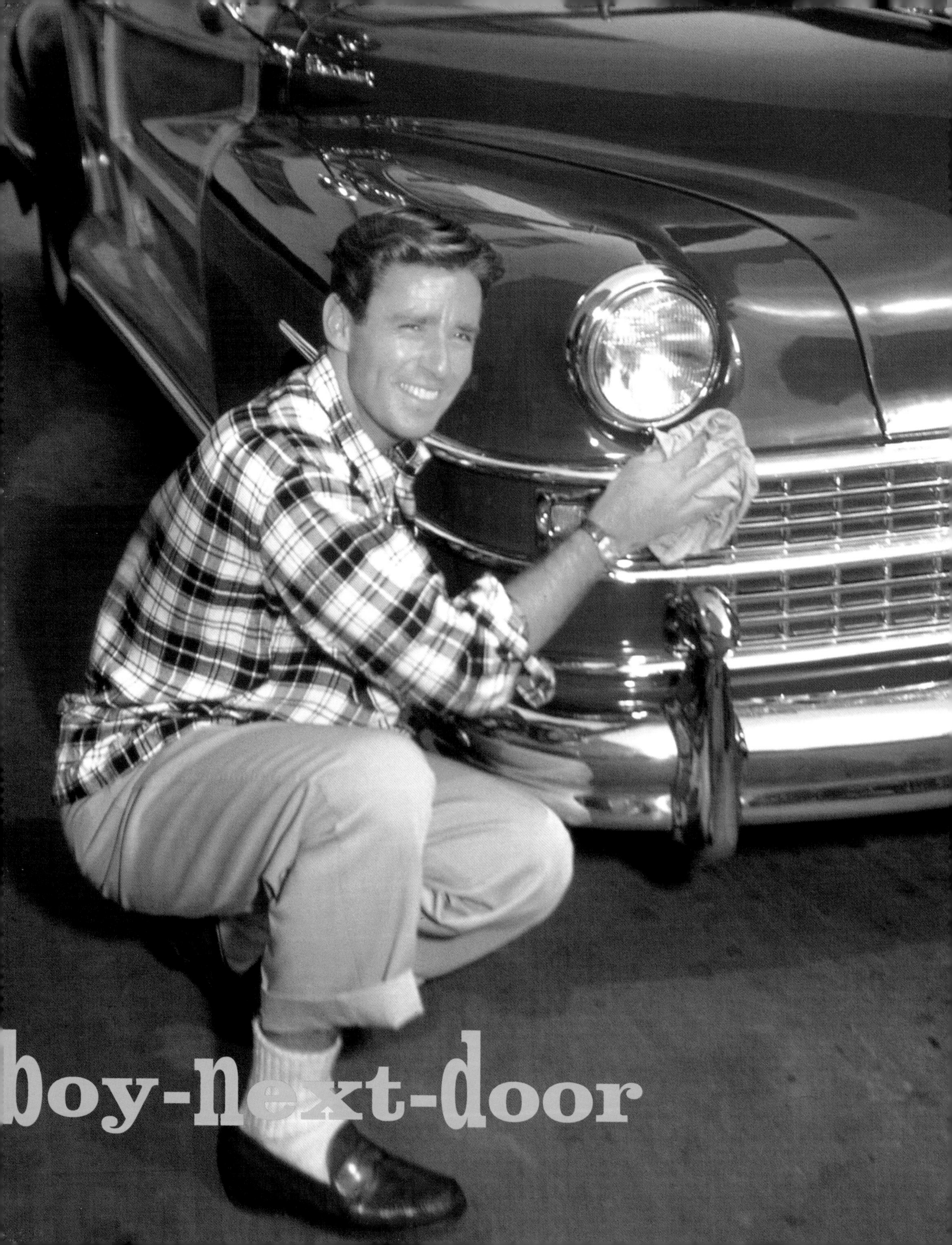

boy-next-door

Who is the "boy-next-door"?
Well, he'd be good-looking (herein being a very good place where the word "cute" is applicable), and up to, but *never* surpassing the level of "handsome," because no one that attractive is supposed to live "next door." (If he was, he couldn't qualify just based on his accessibility and would have to look for another title.) Furthermore, having an ounce of "prettiness" about him doesn't work either, simply because of his lack of hyper-masculine (nee "butch" or "he-man") traits would tend to leave him wide open for suspicion, and we *know* where that can lead. He'd also have a kind heart and thoughtful nature, work out well in a pinch, and always be there when you needed him. Not surprisingly, a favorite of your parents. Now in matters pertaining to the *physical*, one needn't worry about our "boy scout," because sexual aggression is not

part of his makeup. Besides, that would make him a "wolf," and he's definitely more the "puppy" type. Interestingly, he can be quite well-educated, with institutions of higher learning a familiar "home-away-from-home" for our learned fellow. Words like "bookish" are quite often used to describe him, that and terms like "soft-spoken" and "well-behaved." Given the option, do you think many men would like to be considered so middle-of-the-road? Possibly, if for the very reason that the "boy-next-door" is the only group that seems to grow old gracefully; since their looks were never paramount, they seem to have less to lose, and in many cases become even more attractive with the maturing of years (the "matinee idol"-types always living in mortal fear of losing theirs). Now who wouldn't want that!?

left
Peter Lawford (1923–84)
Dazzling of smile, tanned and dimpled, Lawford was the perfect "college boy" who turned every coed's head, and supersophisticated romantic out squiring some wide-eyed American dame. Well-suited in *Good News* (1947), *Easter Parade* (1948), and *Royal Wedding* (1951). (Kobal)

right, top
Van Johnson (b. 1916)
To many of his generation (as well as today), Johnson is the definition of "boy-next-door." Bestowed as such, no doubt, because of the accessibility of his looks and the good-natured ease of his personality (although professionally he has done much to shed the youthful veneer). Check out the "voiceless Sinatra" (so named for his effect on '40s bobbysoxers) in *In the Good Old Summertime* (1949) for old-fashioned fun, *Caine Mutiny* (1954) for a departure, and *Divorce, American Style* (1967) for some laughs. (Kobal)

right, bottom
Robert Walker (1918–51)
Here was our pubescent neighbor with a decided twist. Walker was often on-screen as the adorable, fallible male lead; offscreen his life was tumultuous. Married to actress Jennifer Jones, they were to costar in *Since You Went Away* (1944) while in the process of separating (and she already intimately involved with the producer, and soon husband-to-be, David O. Selznick). Prone to fits of anxiety and alcoholism (which led to a 1948 arrest), Walker had to be sedated "for frazzled nerves" while shooting his last movie, *My Son John*, dying while under the medication. Finest filmed moments: *The Clock* (1945) and Hitchcock's classic *Strangers on a Train* (1951), playing the now-so-obviously-gay murderer, Bruno. (Kobal)

"The really smart actor (or model) will know it's a role they're playing, and not take themselves or their looks too seriously away from the camera."
-- Jim Moore

One must often be leery of becoming involved with the "preppy," for even though he walks in "fun-loving" casual finery, frequently festooned with red sailboats and blue scottie dogs, his clothes may be the only *soft* thing about him. Unutterably handsome though he may be, it seems years of preparatory school has left him bereft of emotion and *hard* as the columns that stand before its entrance.

preppy

The "frat boy" can be a lot of fun, as long as you can get him away from his "brothers," and those ubiquitous kegs. Always up for a good time, the only problem is "Mr. Cute-as-a-Button" never remembers a *thing* about it the next morning. They usually grow up to be "yuppies" (if you call that growing up), and are known to have marvelous taste in suspenders, patterned socks, and cologne. Warning: They are typically not very good dancers, so keep them off the dance floor if you can.

from left to right

Andrew McCarthy (b. 1962)
Quite adorable founding member of the '80s "Brat Pack." Cutest on film in *Class* (1983), *Pretty in Pink* (1986), among others. (*Everett Collection*)

Chris O'Donnell (b. 1970)
Recent addition to "superhunk" status, after doing "wonders" for a polyurethene suit in two *Batman* films, O'Donnell had his film debut way back in 1990, in *Men Don't Leave*. Best feature: Watch him in costume in one of those "bat flicks" to find out. (*Everett Collection*)

Matt Damon (b. 1970)
Such a recent addition to the fold, he wasn't in any of my reference books. Nevertheless, this "golden boy" snagged kudos and an Oscar (with fellow "stud-muffin," Ben Affleck) for penning the screenplay of their hit, *Good Will Hunting* (1997). (*Kobal*)

Woody Harrelson (b. 1961)
Starting out as the self-named, affable bartender in the TV show "Cheers" (1985-92), Woody's gone on to greater acclaim on film, most notably in his Oscar-nominated turn as pornmeister Larry Flynt, in *The People vs. Larry Flynt* (1996). Best visual: a fake Times Square, NY, billboard ad, in Calvin Klein underwear, for the film *The Cowboy Way* (1994). Gives new meaning to that first name. (*Kobal*)

Mark Harmon (b. 1951)
Pegged as one of the sexiest men of the '80s (and we agree), Harmon began his career as the quintessential, handsome "yuppie" even before the term was invented. Maturing (with appropriate grey hair) into a fine actor, Mark was once a football All-American (for UCLA), and has been married to actress Pam Dawber since 1987. Eeriest role: as Ted Bundy (the serial killer) in the telefilm "Deliberate Stranger" (1987). (*Kobal*)

James Dean (1931–55) Instantly elevated to "legend" upon his death, little can be said of Dean's career that hasn't been already. Almost *too* pretty and *too* sensitive to be a leading man, it is the knowledge we have (now) of his real life (then) that gives his few screen roles such poignancy and immediacy. And it is doubtful he could have sustained his career much longer anyway, given his penchant for "fast living." Oscar-nominated posthumously for *East of Eden* (1955) and *Giant* (1956), his costar Sal Mineo (from the homoerotically charged *Rebel Without a Cause*) once said of Dean, "We were never lovers, but we could have been." (*MPTV Archives*)

Marlon Brando (b. 1924) Has two of the sexiest moments on film, in the same movie—*A Streetcar Named Desire* (1951)—and a rent t-shirt plays a major factor. Actors never acted like that before and they weren't suppose to have bodies like that, either! Much to the chagrin of censors and (not-too-secret) delight of moviegoers across the globe. This method-acting Oscar winner (for 1954's *On The Waterfront* and 1972's *The Godfather*) has often been called America's greatest film star. Biggest irony: ballooning to upwards of three-hundred pounds, forever erasing his once spectacular physique. (*MPTV Archives*)

Montgomery Clift (1920–66) Along with Brando and Dean, considered the best of the "new breed" of post-WW II actors. Although it must be said, that out of the three, Clift easily played the most "sensitive" roles. At times exquisitely beautiful, Clift endured such a tortured, self-hating existence (with his sexuality playing a major role) that its finality seems in retrospect almost prophetic. Thankfully, we have his films to remember him by. Some of my favorites: *The Heiress* (1949), *A Place in the Sun* (1951), and *From Here to Eternity* (1953). Best physical features: all of them. (*Kobal*)

He's the "rebel" who will take you to places you've never even dreamed existed, but hold on tight—it's going to be a bumpy ride. Often the beautiful brute (in a soiled tee), he's surprisingly tender. But though he can be charming and captivating, he's never completely comfortable in your company. But this unrest lies somewhere deep within *him*, not you, and though you try as hard as you can there's no penetrating the invisible wall that surrounds him (and his heart). So you savor the few moments you have together, for you know you can never call him your own.

"In their dress, grooming, and demeanor, Brando, Dean and Clift broke all the rules. Nowadays no one even knows what those rules were."
—Amy Fine Collins

the Outsider

bad boy

Nick Adams (1931–68)
This "hunky" JD (as in juvenile delinquent) never quite graduated to the "big room" (despite his Oscar nom for 1963's *Twilight of Honor*), possibly because his too-boyish good looks (and rabble-rousing) prevented it. Died of a drug overdose. (*MacFadden/Corbis-Bettmann*)

Anthony Perkins (1932–92)
Oscar-nominated for *Friendly Persuasion* (1956), though best-remembered for his role as the psychotic killer, Norman Bates, in Hitchcock's *Psycho* (1960). However, keep an eye out for *Pretty Poison* (1968) to see more of the dark underbelly of this handsome "loner." Dying of AIDS, he was yet another Hollywood "pretty boy" whose real life was kept well away from the public eye. (*Kobal*)

Avoid the "bad boy" because he's just trouble. But you can change him, right? The others don't understand him like you do. They don't see what you see. Not only can you sense the hurt child, but the great man yearning to get his chance at success and make his mark on this no-good world. But there is something more to it than samaritan intentions, isn't there? He's really far too attractive to let the thought of a little danger keep you away. So why not walk on the wild side for a spell, until things get too hot to handle.

Dean Stockwell (b. 1936)
Enjoyed a successful spate of childhood roles (including his debut in 1945's *Anchors Aweigh*), did well as a handsome, if troubled, teen-slash-young adult (in *Compulsion* [1959] and *Sons and Lovers* [1960]), disappearing for a while before emerging as a fine, though quirky, character actor in recent years. Today's audiences should know his *Blue Velvet* (1986), *Married to the Mob* (1988), for which he received an Academy Award nomination, and as Al, opposite "hunka-bunka" Scott Bakula, in the series "Quantum Leap" (1989-93). (*MacFadden/Corbis-Bettmann*)

John Saxon (b. 1935)
This "brooding babe" was once a male model (no, I don't believe it!) before turning to acting and screaming female (and I'm sure a few silent male) fans in a number of teen-skewed films of the late '50s. Has an enormous body of work (and body, too!) that unfortunately did not make him a bigger star. Appeared in "The Doctors" segments of the 1969-73 series, "The Bold Ones." (*Kobal*)

"Good-looking men are like cotton candy; though not necessarily good for you, you've just got to have it."
— Thomas Hoving

man trouble

He might be a grown man now, but the "bad boy" never looses that edge. The one that keeps *you* on guard all the time, always on your best behavior, for fear of offending *him*. And you never know when he's gonna slug you, rob a convenience store, gamble all your money away or find someone else. It seems all these thyroidal thugs learned up the river was how to lift weights (and *so* well, it's no wonder you stick around).

clockwise, from left to right

Sean Penn (b. 1960)
As much maligned for his offscreen high jinks as he is acclaimed for his on-screen talent, this "dude" exudes sex appeal, literally, out of every pore. Finally received some validation for his acting ability with an Oscar nom for *Dead Man Walking* (1995). Once notoriously married (as you well know) to Madonna (1985-89), now to actress Robin Wright. (*Everett Collection*)

Brad Pitt (b. 1963)
"Stud-muffin" whose bare derriere (in 1991's *Thelma and Louise*) sent pleasant shivers down many a viewer's spines. No way could Geena Davis have resisted that! Although a far more serious and gifted actor than those golden moments would allow. Now senior member of Hollywood's recently dubbed "Frat Pack," Pitt is notoriously guarded about his private life (and parts, re: *Playgirl* magazine) feeling that the more you know about an actor, the more they become a personality and less a star. Academy Award nomination for *12 Monkeys* (1995). (*Everett Collection*)

Keanu Reeves (b. 1965)
Possibly *not* as talented as his beautific brethren, this dark-eyed "Adonis" has been fending off the "teen idol" handle since his breakthrough in *Bill and Ted's Excellent Adventure* (1989), but has found it even harder to do so after his "studly" turn in the megahit *Speed* (1994). Nevertheless, his acting has improved with time, even as he continues to grow handsomer with every appearance. Possible best film, so far: as a gay hustler in *My Own Private Idaho* (1991). (*Kobal*)

Ethan Hawke (b. 1970)
Boyishly good-looking star, who seems destined to become a very fine actor, indeed. Most recently in *Gattaca* (1997) and the remake of *Great Expectations* (1998). (*Everett Collection*)

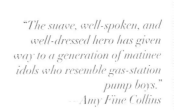

"The suave, well-spoken, and well-dressed hero has given way to a generation of matinee idols who resemble gas-station pump boys."
— *Amy Fine Collins*

right

Henry "Hank" Fonda (1905–82)
As a young male star, he was almost too pretty; however, subsequent maturity mellowed his looks into a fine accessible attractiveness. Adept in comedy, drama, and romance, on film, stage, and television, Fonda also found time to be a Hollywood "liberal" (much to the chagrin of his good friend, conservative Jimmy Stewart), as well as father to Peter and Jane, and grandfather to Bridget (although there is some debate as to how *good* a dad he really was). Once married to actress Margaret Sullavan, Fonda's film debut was *A Farmer Takes A Wife* (1935), finally winning the Oscar for *On Golden Pond* (1981). Look out for *The Grapes of Wrath* (1940), *Lady Eve* (1941), *Mister Roberts* (1955), reprising his Broadway role, and *The Best Man* (1964). (*MacFadden/Corbis-Bettmann*)

far right

James "Jimmy" Stewart (1908–97)
Though not a "heartthrob" in the truest sense, looks certainly played a major role in his lifelong popularity, and Stewart ended up becoming one of cinema's finest and most likable stars. An enduring icon, he was also archly conservative (causing a mild riff between he and pal, "Hank" Fonda). Oscar winner for *The Philadelphia Story* in 1940 (nominated five times), he made the tricky transitions from "boy-next-door" to "leading man" to "beloved patriarch" with relative ease. Medal of Honor winner, too, in 1985–this country's highest civilian award. Some of my favorite Stewart films: *Harvey* (1950), *Rear Window* (1954) with the divine Grace Kelly, *Vertigo*, and *Bell, Book, and Candle* (both 1958 and both with the sultry Kim Novak). (*MPTV Archives*)

"Men and women are so much better off today than they were when our parents were young. We discuss things and consider each other more as equals. And now we can talk openly about our physical attraction for each other, where it had to be kept within the sexes before."
— Claudia Schiffer

Though the sound—"everyman"—is not glamourous (and the point is it's not supposed to be), that doesn't stop them from being quite attractive members of the male sex. The idea is to take all men (everywhere) and average them out by height, weight, hair color, habits, job description, pant size—well you get the gist of it—sort of like throwing them all into a blender (and haven't we all wanted to do that at one time or another) and out the top pours this guy who's just cute enough, smart enough, and sweet enough to satisfy practically everyone. However, this "normalcy" doesn't mean he is a man void of superlatives. More than likely he is an upstanding citizen, outstanding father (or father figure), and understanding lover. Fellow celluloid members of this fraternal order of good guys include Mr. Jack Lemmon and, the newest inductee, Mr. Tom Hanks.

everyman

the Swell

left
Douglas Fairbanks, Jr. (b. 1909) Nearly as handsome and debonair as a man could get, this self-effacing luminary has never thought of himself as a (style) icon, despite the overwhelming opinions of the viewing public. Once married to Joan Crawford (1929-33), Fairbanks, for a long time, lived under the "swashbuckling" shadow of his famed father before developing into a star in his own right. Well-liked in England, where he was knighted, Douglas hosted his own television anthology series, aptly titled "Douglas Fairbanks Presents" (1953-56). *(Kobal)*

starting from near right, top
Ray Milland
(1907–87, Reginald Truscott-Jones) Superbly attractive, always nattily dressed star (and sometimes director) of dozens of films. Oscar winner for Billy Wilder's classic *The Lost Weekend* (1945), the scheming husband in Hitchcock's *Dial M for Murder* (1954), and Ryan O'Neal's father in *Love Story* (1970). *(Kobal)*

Joseph Cotten (1905–94) Sophisticated and disarming, this onetime drama critic came to immediate fame via his role (as a drama critic) in *Citizen Kane* (1941). A huge star of the '40s (*The Magnificent Ambersons* [1942], *Shadow of a Doubt* [1943], *Gaslight* [1944], and *Portrait of Jennie* [1948]), Cotten's "star" began to slip in the '50s. He never really cared for his profession, because it was, in his own words, too "easy to do." Interesting tidbit: played the lead on Broadway, opposite Katharine Hepburn in *The Philadelphia Story* (1939). Most distinctive feature: that hair. *(MPTV Archives)*

Fredric March
(1897–1975, Ernest Frederick McIntyre Bickel) Can't imagine why he'd want to change his name! Smartly handsome, March managed to segue from romantic lead to distinguished character actor with great aplomb. Won two Oscars, the first for Mamoulian's *Dr. Jekyll and Mr. Hyde* (1932) and his second for *The Best Years of Our Lives* (1946). Most telling change of facial features: the addition of a moustache for the second half of his career. *(Kobal)*

Dana Andrews (1909–92) Volatile, "hunkish" lead of '40s films, especially good playing hard-boiled types, such as the swaggering detective in the classic noir pic, *Laura* (1944). However, with his slightly impassive demeanor, his career did not progress as well as he would have liked. Brother of actor Steve Forrest. *(Kobal)*

Tyrone Power (1913–58) Huge romantic idol of the late '30s and '40s, Power's incursion into acting is not accidental, as both his father and grandfather (as well as his own son) were and are all actors. (Incidentally, they were all named Tyrone, too, though it is doubtful who the most famous one is.) Exquisitely dark-featured, this "pretty boy" was a star by 1937, and though his career was neatly bisected by the war, he returned with more maturity (in looks and acting) to continued fame. This onetime screen "Zorro" appeared in many noteworthy films, including his "swan song," Billy Wilder's *Witness for the Prosecution* (1958). *(Kobal)*

"For a time, I left pictures and went into the service. In the beginning the men would try to 'put me in my place.' They assumed that, as a movie star, I expected preferential treatment. Well, I endured all their schoolboy tricks, and proved to them I was as 'tough' as they were." – Douglas Fairbanks, Jr.

Believe me, we haven't seen a swell in years. This spiffily dressed fellow went out with gloves and hats. Sad, because just the sound of it— "here come a coupla' swells"— is just *too* stylish for words. Bear in mind, that these words spoke of "gentle" men of great social standing, too. But that's another breed of male that bit the dust eons ago. A list of dashing "swellegants" who couldn't make this page: Joel McCrea, John Lund, Gilbert Roland, David Niven, Franchot Tone, Cornel Wilde, to name but a few.

Nowhere is it written that in order to be *funny* you have to look the part. Precisely the opposite seems to be the case. Though a chiseled chin may be too humorless, a pearly smile, a couple of dimples, and a glimmer in your eye may be just enough to catch their attention before covering it up with a lamp shade. In fact, if you stop guys like Jim Carrey from spinning around long enough, a real "hunk" comes into focus. The same can be said for firebrands like Robin Williams and all the rest of these cuddly clowns.

near right, middle
Steve Martin (b. 1945)
Perfect example of where a bit of goofiness and pratfalling can distract the viewer away from a rather sublime exterior. Put another way, if *The Jerk* (1979) had remained immobile for more than a few moments his cover would be blown, exposing a very good-looking fellow. Best film role: playing himself *and* Lily Tomlin's incarnation in *All of Me* (1984). Emmy winner as a comedy cowriter for "The Smothers Brothers Comedy Hour" (1969). Also had a top-twenty music hit with the irreverent "King Tut" in 1978. Best physical feature: the salt-and-pepper hair. (*MPTV Archives*)

middle right, top
Harold Lloyd (1893–1971)
Quite possibly, Lloyd's signature black, horn-rimmed eyeglasses (which he supposedly did not need) were used as much to camouflage his handsomeness, as they were used to imply that people were more fallible (and therefore, funnier) if they wore them. This cinematic "nice boy" is widely considered America's premier comic genius and pioneer of physical comedy. Most famous film scene: hanging from a clock hand in *Safety Last* (1923). Little-known act of perseverance: lost two fingers in a 1920 explosion, but continued doing his own stunts for the duration of his career. 1952 Special Oscar for being a "master comedian and good citizen." (*Everett Collection*)

middle right, bottom
Eddie Murphy (b. 1961)
A brilliant and "bad boy" handsome comedic supertalent, whose characterizations on "Saturday Night Live" (from the early '80s) led to even bigger success on the big screen. His films took a bit of a nosedive in the late '80s, but rebounded quite nicely with the smash *The Nutty Professor* (1996), playing five members of his own family. A music hit parader, too, with his number-two single, "Party All the Time" (1985). (*Everett Collection*)

far right
Leslie Nielsen (b. 1922)
Starting out as a romantic lead, Nielsen's hair had to turn white (and he had to cross over into middle age) in order to be taken seriously as an actor, albeit a comedic one. And it is those deftly handled farcical turns that have kept him in the spotlight for the last twenty years now. However, if you want to see him at his most "babe-like," take a gander at his sleek physique in *Forbidden Planet* (1956) and *Tammy and the Bachelor* (1957). Best physical features today: that still grand proboscis and, for an older guy, a great chest! (*Everett Collection*)

funny guy

Villain

The villain is not necessarily a grown-up version of the "bad boy," nor is he the opposite of the "funny guy," lacking in a sense of humor. He is in a *class* by himself. We know we're suppose to despise him, but it's very hard. It's that Dracula thing, where you're repelled *and* attracted at the same time (however, it helps if the "winged-one" looks like Gary Oldman or Frank Langella). Pyschologically speaking, somewhere way down in our subconscious we've allowed our carnal thoughts to become ensnared with our mean thoughts (you know, things like letting the elevator close on your chatty neighbor), mainly because most of us had been taught early that sex is a bad thing. So anytime anyone is really evil (or withholding) this dysfunctional side kicks in and we run *to* it instead of away. But to be honest, sometimes the scoundrel is so downright gorgeous, you can't help but fall from grace. Besides, handsome as he invariably is, the "good guy" can be a little dull.

left
Basil Rathbone (1892–1967)
A menacing, and yet at times alluring, though always suave presence in dozens of features. At once the intellectually attractive (and unquestionably the screen's most satisfying) Sherlock Holmes, then dangerously appealing as possibly the best real "bad boy" on film. Tony Award for *The Heiress* (1947). Twice nominated for (Best Supporting Actor) Oscars–*Romeo and Juliet* (1936) and *If I Were King* (1938)–this saturnine sycophant was rumored to be quite a "beast" in bed, too! (*Everett Collection*)

above
Vincent Price (1911–93)
Who would have guessed that Price, before he became known as the "Prince of Horror," would have started out as such a "pretty boy"? But don't take my word for it, for further evidence sneak a peek at his muscled countenance in the classic, shadowy thriller, *Laura* (1944) (incidentally, a film rife with homoerotic innuendo). Then maybe take a look at his small, but "meaty," role in *Leave Her To Heaven* (1945). This dashing possessor of a Masters Degree in Art History (from London University), was also once the art-buying consultant for, of all places, Sears and Roebuck! (*Kobal*)

right
George Sanders (1906–72)
This beauteous Russian-born bounder made many a costar miserable on- (and off-) screen, but did it so elegantly you'd have to forgive him. Once famously wed to Zsa Zsa Gabor (from 1949-54), he won the Oscar for playing the scoundrel-critic, Addison DeWitt, in *All About Eve* (1950). With just the sound of his voice, this "ne'er-do-well" made many a film infinitely more watchable. Best title of anything he was associated with: *Memoirs of a Professional Cad* (his 1960 autobiography). (*Everett Collection*)

"I know that we make ourselves 'slaves' of physical ideals that are mostly unattainable. The result is a great deal of self-loathing. The good news is that affection cancels ugly threats."
— Isabella Rossellini

The actor-type *can* take himself a little too seriously. You know, all for art and that sort of thing. Well, at least he got over that early hammy and histrionic period of screen performing (from the silents through the '30s), laden with characters so hyberbolic they were practically crashing through the ceiling. Not that they were disingenuous, but no one's life is that tragic or heroic. Fortunately, that all came to somewhat of an end with the war, forcing the industry to handle their projects a bit more realistically. The emergence of color film had a hand in this changeover too, as throughout the '40s and '50s black and white films stayed the more dramatic, while color (though in the beginning was used for more lavish productions) became, understandably, a natural setting for actors (other than a world filled with only shades of grey). Notably, actors themselves changed, both physically and philosophically (although there were always exceptions, like Spencer Tracy and Humphrey Bogart, who played themselves magnificently for decades). We went from the depression-escapist William Powells (in the '30s), to power propagandist Robert Mitchums and honest idealist Gregory Pecks (in the '40s), to a mixed bag of method and non-method actors in the '50s. In particular, it was the Adler-aided actor of the time, Brando, and company (though not necessarily less *dramatic*), who came across as decidedly more human. So with their newfound popularity the Clifts begat the Newmans, and on down the line, through Beatty, McQueen, Redford, Hoffman, DeNiro, Pacino, Ford, Hanks, and so on. However, in the context of this book which is supposed to be about looks, there are very few actors who have managed to successfully separate how they presented their *craft* from the way they presented *themselves*. And it may be impossible to do so. As earnest, heartfelt, and moving Tracy's or Bogart's performance is, the camera would always focus more attention on the Gables and Grants.

"Reality is very important (in film), but a certain amount of naivete and innocence is missing. I know you can't go back to that, but it was sweet for what it was."
-- Tab Hunter

dandy

Leslie Howard (1893–1943)
This foppishly pretty "boy-man" was the screen's original Henry Higgins, in Shaw's *Pygmalion* (1938), though his most famous roles (this side of the Atlantic) must be as the ever-so-slightly "fey" hero of *The Scarlet Pimpernel* (1935) and Ashley Wilkes, the unrequited love-interest of Scarlett O'Hara, in *Gone With The Wind* (1939). Immensely popular on both sides of the "pond," Howard was tragically killed when his plane was shot down en route from Lisbon to London, during WW II. (Evidentally, the Nazis were said to have believed that Winston Churchill was also present on the flight. Obviously he was not.) Interestingly, the English public mourned Howard's death to a degree that would not be equaled *until* that of the famed prime minister. *(MPTV Archives)*

Ralph Fiennes (b. 1962)
Possessing almost "radiant" attractiveness, Fiennes's fine features were enough to make a supersmash out of the slightly ponderous *The English Patient* (1996). Amazingly, too, he came to prominence as the boorish, bellied Nazi in *Schindler's List* (1993). Best "look": as Charles Van Doren in *The Quiz Show* (1994). Two Oscar noms for *List* and *Patient*. A Tony for 1995's *Hamlet*. *(Everett Collection)*

Daniel Day-Lewis (b. 1957)
Running the gamut from hapless suitor (in 1985's *A Room With A View*) to "beefy" frontiersman (in 1992's *Last of the Mohicans*), Day-Lewis is an actor of incredible range. The fact that he can be at times painfully pretty, however, makes the journey that much easier. Extra "fabulous" in *My Beautiful Laundrette* (1985) with that bi-colored hair thing goin' on. Oscar for *My Left Foot* (1989). For you trivia buffs: starred in the 1982 British stage version of *Another Country*. Hmmm. *(Everett Collection)*

Rex Harrison (1908–90)
Dubbed "Sexy-Rexy" by gossip columnists because of his scandalous lifestyle (part of it involving the suicide of actress Carole Landis) and its effects on fans, this dashing, urbane, and slightly roguish star (first in England and then stateside) found his greatest success (and an Oscar and Tony) for his incarnation of Henry Higgins in the Lerner and Loewe musical *My Fair Lady*. Knighted in 1989. *(Kobal)*

Laurence Olivier (1907–89)
If for nothing else, Olivier brought watchability (and sex appeal) to Shakespeare. Nine-time Oscar nominee, Laurence was pretty before he was handsome, and handsome before he was distinguished, all the while playing memorable characters like Heathcliff in *Wuthering Heights* (1939), Max DeWinter in *Rebecca* (1940), and the Bard's *Hamlet* (1948). Married to actresses Jill Esmond, Vivien Leigh, and Joan Plowright, his memory of late has had to contend with speculation on his supposed bisexuality. But regardless of whether he liked "oysters or snails," Olivier's impact on the acting profession goes unquestioned. Knighted in 1947, he was made a Lord in 1971, then in 1975 London's Theatre Awards (England's version of the Tony) were renamed "Olivier" in his honor. *(MPTV Archives)*

"The way a man looks physically and dresses (especially in a suit) can be quite commanding, because it implies order when all else around him is in disorder."
— Geoffrey Beene

The poet. The fabulous fop. So sadly missing from our midst. He enchanted us with his entrancing smile and beguiled us with his bewitching beauty. But this man-boy was no mere vision in velvet and lace, cloaked in the fog of night, he was passion's sensitive soldier waiting to caress you with a gentle kiss.

When it comes to *amour*, Hollywood has always felt safer with casting a man with an accent. That's not to say American actors can't play romantic leads, it's just that some of them look silly trying. I mean how awkward is Charlton Heston or John Wayne when they try to be passionate on-screen? The feeling is, why not leave all that lovemaking stuff to the men who invented it? Besides, we make out all-right. How many Frenchmen do you know that make good action heroes?

near right, top
Rossano Brazzi (1916–94)
In the '50s, Brazzi did more for Italo-American relations than both governments put together. At a time when films found it increasingly necessary to serve as a type of travelogue for ticket-buyers (especially capitalizing on new wide-screen processes) to entice attendance, Rossano's "Latin lover" looks almost stole the show. Yet, though his continental bravado adorned over one hundred films, this onetime lawyer truly appeared in only a handful that are memorable: *The Barefoot Contessa* (1954) with an equally lovely Ava Gardner, *Three Coins in the Fountain* (1954) competing with the grandeur of Rome, *Summertime* (1955) overflowing with Venetian splendor, and *South Pacific* (1958) with his singing dubbed, looking tanned and *magnifique*. Best feature: among others, his accent! (*MPTV Archives*)

near right, bottom
Yul Brynner (1915–85)
The only major star to reach the top without anything on his! (And I am sorry, but Patrick Stewart, though veeery sexy, isn't there yet!) This part-Gypsy, all-male superdynamo played his famous role of the King of Siam from *The King and I* on stage over 4,600 times, including the film version (1956), a role that netted him one of those coveted "golden" statuettes. Once a trapeze artist, Brynner brought a virile quality to his many screen roles that was due, no doubt, to his shiny pate. (Giving fuel to the notion that bald men are sexier.) Most interesting, though not necessarily good, look: with a head full of hair in *Port of New York* (1949), his film debut. (*MacFadden/Corbis-Bettmann*)

Louis Jourdan (b. 1919)
Expected to be a much bigger star than he became, Jourdan found it hard to get roles playing anything more than the cultured, international "lover" types. But he did those so well, so who could blame the casting director? Lovely to look at in *Letter to an Unknown Woman* (1948), *Madame Bovary* (1949), and *Gigi* (1959), as if it were hard to do so in his other films (not!), Jourdan was, amazingly, part of the French Underground during WW II, before his American debut in Alfred Hitchcock's *The Paradine Case* (1948). (*Kobal*)

the Continental

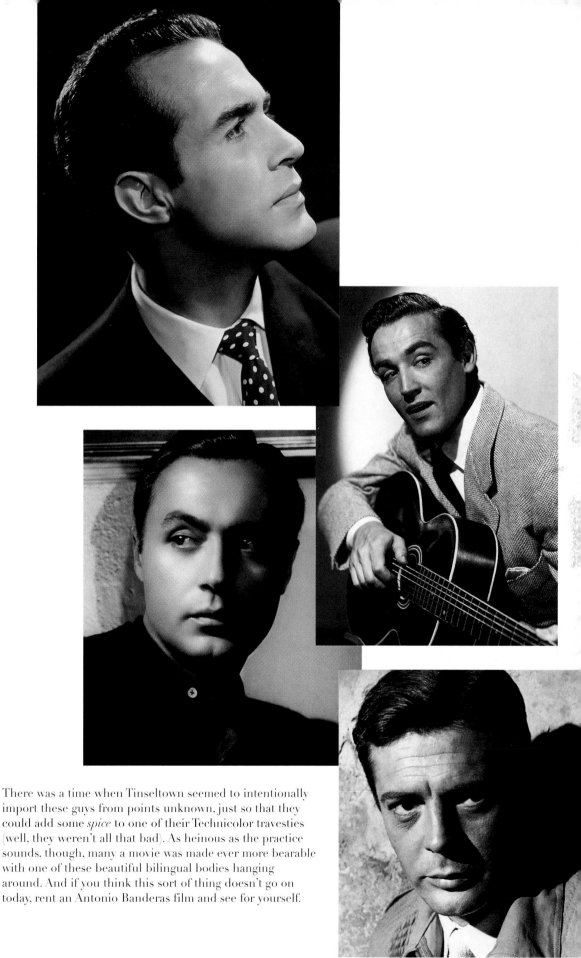

Jacques Sernas (b. 1925)
Superbly beautiful of face and body, a relatively unknown Sernas was picked from dozens
of hopefuls to play the male lead (of Paris) in
the 1956 epic, *Helen of Troy.* Though he fit the
role perfectly, his acting left much to be
desired, and at the time made only one other
Hollywood film (1955's *Jump into Hell*) before
fading from the spotlight. However his best
role, among many "gladiator" films, may be his
small part as the fading matinee idol in
Fellini's *La Dolce Vita* (1960). Amazingly, much
of his on-screen histrionics may have been
culled from some of his own real-life
drama–during WW II he was imprisoned for
over a year at Buchenwald. Most telling sign
of the times: his makeup-covered "pecs" in
Helen of Troy. (*MPTV Archives*)

Ricardo Montalban (b. 1920)
This Emmy winner (for TV's "How the West
Was Won," Part II) was one of Hollywood's
two most famous "Latin lovers" of the late
'40s and early '50s (the other being Fernando
Lamas). However, Montalban fought very
hard to break from the typecasting to varying
degrees of success, though as the star of television's long-running "Fantasy Island" (1978-
84), he was a resounding hit. Best look: dis-
playing his magnificent body, whenever and
wherever he could, even in Kabuki makeup
(in 1957's *Sayonara*). Best line: "Fine,
Corinthian leather." (*MPTV Archives*)

Vittorio Gassman (b. 1922)
Though he has always been a much bigger
star in his home country (Italy), that hadn't
stopped Gassman from making sporadic
attempts at fame on American shores. Most
notably during his two-year marriage to
actress Shelly Winters (1952-54) and a short-
lived contract with MGM (resulting in his role
opposite Elizabeth Taylor in 1954's *Rhapsody*).
With his arched brows askance, a wickedly
handsome Vittorio often played the roué,
though his sharp handling of comedy has
unquestionably extended his marketability.
(*MPTV Archives*)

Charles Boyer (1897–1978)
One of the few foreign "imports" who
became as big a sensation in the States as he
was in his own homeland. And what a sensation! The screen's "Great Lover," Boyer
became the standard by which every
American woman (and I am sure, man)
would forever judge a worthy paramour. (But
how could anyone compete with that face
and that voice!) The quintessence of the
romantic Gaul, Boyer was nominated for
Oscars four times. Though never winning, he
was given a Special Award in 1942 for his
"cultural achievements" in solidifying wartime
French and American relations. To see what
all the fuss was about, watch *Love Affair*
(1939) and *Gaslight* (1944), as two diverse
selections of many screen appearances. Sadly,
he took his own life only two days after the
death of his wife Pat (whom he was married
to since 1934). (*MPTV Archives*)

Marcello Mastroianni (1923–96)
Beginning in 1947, Marcello gradually gained
worldwide acclaim through such noted films
as *La Dolce Vita* (1959), *Divorce, Italian Style*
(1961), *8 1/2* (1962), and *A Special Day*
(1977). Very rarely seen in an American picture, his career and reputation as a superb
actor has not suffered for it in the slightest. In
fact, to the contrary, his fame grew as he
became the distillation of the sophisticated,
urbane European man. Also one of the few
actors (in foreign-speaking roles) to be nominated for an Academy Award, and this he did
three times. Once a prisoner during WW II,
this movie "playboy" escaped only to remain
in hiding (in a Venice attic) for the duration of
the war. (*Everett Collection*)

There was a time when Tinseltown seemed to intentionally
import these guys from points unknown, just so that they
could add some *spice* to one of their Technicolor travesties
(well, they weren't all that bad). As heinous as the practice
sounds, though, many a movie was made ever more bearable
with one of these beautiful bilingual bodies hanging
around. And if you think this sort of thing doesn't go on
today, rent an Antonio Banderas film and see for yourself.

Though this knight in shining armor is more likely to show up in fairy tales than he is during your moment of greatest distress, that hasn't stopped us from inventing (and re-inventing) the guy and waiting for him to show. (Although a lot of people feel good examples of this dashing deliverer are fading fast.) Though he may be a bit lofty (and often too right-wing) at times, it's nice to dream that there is such a handsome hero out there, as long as he behaves within reason.

hero

anti-hero

Just because he has "anti" in front of his name doesn't mean you couldn't count on him or wouldn't want him on your side. Really the only major difference between him and a plain old hero is that this guy doesn't play by the rules (which is of course the main reason why so many disciplined people are scared by him). But rules are meant to be broken (especially the bad ones). Anyway, if the ends do justify the means, then what are a few busted-up cars and hearts, as long as this pleasing protagonist saves the day.

The name "lady-killer" shouldn't be taken literally, but you already knew that. The term is more slang for someone who "slays" you with their astonishing good looks. It comes as no surprise then, that it is well-suited to the amorously attractive anti-heroes of film *noir*, a genre of movie that made shadows sexy and was rife with the still-warm bodies of countless "femme fatales" who finally met their match.

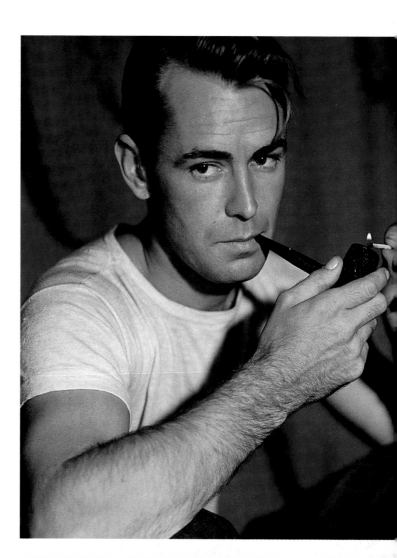

left
Steve McQueen (1930–80)
Somewhat self-destructive on-screen and off, McQueen's enormous popularity drew less from his acting ability (of which Robert Mitchum once said, "lent itself to monotony") and more on his quite original charismatic presence (of which he has an ample supply). Unwittingly too, McQueen became a style "icon" of the late '60s and early '70s; a "Joe Cool," rakish loner who was the perfect visual anecdote for the disillusioned times of his peak popularity. Regardless of the criticism of his talent, McQueen was nominated for an Oscar (for 1966's The Sand Pebbles). Most memorable movie scene: the car chase in Bullitt (1968), which set the standard for all vehicular pursuits that followed. Most mysterious rumors: those that surround his sudden death. (MPTV Archives)

right
Alan Ladd (1913–64)
Very short (especially by Hollywood's standards) at 5' 5", Ladd was reputed to have had to stand atop boxes in order to photograph higher than (or as high as) some of his female costars. (No doubt, in such an egotistical business this must have left him feeling quite insecure.) Nevertheless, he did become a top star beginning (opposite diminutive, but lovely, Veronica Lake) in This Gun For Hire (1942). He showed little of his anxiety on-screen, though that cannot be said of his life off. Playing the two-fisted hero up until his death, at age fifty, Ladd's demise came about with an "accidental" mixture of alcohol and sedatives. What's considered his best film: the somewhat overly symbolic western, Shane (1953). And, if you can find it: a very unusual, especially for the times, shirtless cover of him on Motion Picture magazine (from the mid-'40s). (Kobal)

The "King" of Hollywood, as his contemporaries liked to call him. And to this day, still the acting "man's man" by which all other unwitting gents are judged. Quite undeniably fetching as a young actor (starting in 1924), his career exploded with the success of *It Happened One Night* (1934), a loan-out film which Gable considered a "demotion." (He won the Oscar.) By the time he added his signature moustache (which he kept until his death) in the late '30s, his most acclaimed role, as Rhett Butler in *Gone With the Wind* (1939), seemed merely icing on the cake. Regardless of the unrivalled supremacy of his "reign," by the '50s Gable would work less frequently (as many once-major stars at the time did) and he died in 1960, just months before the birth of his only child, son John. Most interesting impact on popular culture: watching the sales of undershirts plummet, after showing he wore none in the bedroom scene from *It Happened One Night*. *(MPTV Archives)*

At one time, the most dashing and breathtakingly beautiful man to ever grace the silver screen. Swashbuckling films seemed to have been created just for him, so as to frame his sweeping personality. Born in Tasmania (of all places), Flynn's "bad boy" image seemed honed at an early age; he was constantly expelled from schools. Though, despite his ribald and exuberant persona, Flynn was deeply disappointed at being turned down for acceptance into any branch of the armed services (due to a heart defect, slight tuberculosis, and a touch of malaria). Nevertheless, Errol found it easy to stay in trouble, most infamously as the accused (but acquitted) attacker of two teenage girls. The once often used phrase "In like Flynn" stemmed from the resulting publicity. Flynn was rumoured to be both a Nazi-sympathizer and bisexual. Jack Warner (of Warner Bros.) once said of him that, "to the Walter Mittys of the world he was all the heroes in one magnificent, sexy animal package." Charmingly attractive moment: in tights, as Robin in *The Adventures of Robin Hood* (1938). *(Kobal)*

(1904–86, Archibald Alexander Leach) The most debonair of filmdom's leading men, and, more often than not, the one individual singled out as the best example of great style and sophistication. Dark of features, cleft-chinned and surprisingly well-built (especially among his "soft" peers), Grant oozed charm in every role he undertook. And that was regardless of whether he played an angel (in 1947's *The Bishop's Wife*, where this scene still is from), an embattled husband (in 1948's *Mr. Blandings Builds a Dream House*), or an innocent bystander, embroiled in espionage (1958's *North by Northwest*). Not surprisingly, he was one of the few (if possibly the only) actors of his time who never had to make the professional switch from romantic leads to character roles. *(John Springer/Corbis-Bettmann)*

"The thing about beautiful men is that they create a primal longing. One can't seem to tear one's eyes away. When I first saw Cary Grant on the screen, even though I was ten years old, his image was so extraordinary. I wanted more, to stare and stare.

If each of us were to write out a list of the things we wanted in a mate (from personality traits to looks, and so on), chances are there would be some things on your list in common with mine and vice versa, but it is unlikely that they would match exactly. Now, try gathering this information from a whole country full of people. Sound a bit hard? Well, on some level this has been going on for years. Pretty much everything we *see* exists because someone somewhere decided that we liked it, based on examining the evidence (i.e., what we said we liked, liked before, or liked once). Which leads me to the category of "the ideal." Interestingly, every gentleman who fits into this group (and you know who they are), will only please some of the people some of the time. So much for pigeon-holing public taste.

It makes me think of the Sara Teasdale lines 'Oh beauty; are you not enough? Why am I crying after love?'"
—Olivia Goldsmith

thinking Man

Here is the guy where looks, brains, and a heart come together in one glorious, "I wanna' marry that!" package. As good-looking as he is, though, there is still humility to the handsomeness, and this academic is no scolding scholar. When it comes to soul-searching, one need look no further. (However, thankfully, his humanity outreaches his piety.) Amazingly, he comes in all shapes and sizes, and may be more widely available today then he ever has been in the past, a benefit of the "Age of Information," where one can't avoid the truth. From Sam Waterston to Samuel Jackson, Gary Sinise to Sam Shepard, these savvy savants await with open minds and open hearts.

left
Gregory Peck (b. 1916)
If only all "father figures" could be as conscionable (and as attractive) as Peck, the world would be a much nicer place. Became a star during the last years of WW II (in the absence of other comparable male talent) because he was unable to join himself, due to a spinal injury. (However, his striking good looks and superlative talent would have garnered praise at any time.) By the late '40s, after appearing in such socially relevant pictures as *Gentlemen's Agreement* (1947), Peck was well on his way to becoming filmdom's ideal personification of the "thoughtful" moviegoer. An Oscar winner, as Atticus Finch in *To Kill A Mockingbird* (1962), Peck has also been awarded the Medal of Freedom. Best physical feature: those di-i-i-vine eyebrows. Meanest role: as the "sleazy" brother in *Duel in the Sun* (1947). (*MPTV Archives*)

near right, top
Sterling Hayden (1916–86)
Looking like a Nordic God, he was, not surprisingly, drawn to the sea in real life, serving in the marines and the OSS during WW II. Once married to equally stunning Madeleine Carroll (1942-46), his best acting role was as the hood in *The Asphalt Jungle* (1950). An admitted onetime Communist (confessed during the McCarthy era), Hayden never got over the experience, professionally or privately. Also good in *Dr. Strangelove* (1964) and as a "bad" cop in *The Godfather* (1972). (*Kobal*)

near right, middle
Anthony Quinn (b. 1915)
With all the public satyr-like behavior, it's easy to forget that Quinn is quite the accomplished actor with two Best Supporting Actor Oscars to prove it (for 1952's *Viva Zapata!* and 1956's *Lust for Life*). And also, despite the bravado, this burly brute is quite the acclaimed painter, too! (*MPTV Archives*)

middle right, top
Victor Mature (1915–94)
Hollywood's "Samson," both on and off the screen. Was the first of the '40s wartime "beefcakes" and possibly a better actor than the films he was given allowed him to be, though Mature was the last to complain. And, despite all that marvelous brawn, looked great in a suit, too! However, check out *Samson and Delilah* (1949) for a glimpse of all that muscle. (*Kobal*)

middle right, bottom
Jeff Chandler (1918–61, Ira Grossel)
Stolid, prematurely grey-haired lead of mainly action films, most memorably as Cochise in *Broken Arrow* (1950), an interestingly pro-Indian-skewed film for the time. For all his "manliness," he died suddenly from blood poisoning following surgery. (*MacFadden/Corbis-Bettmann*)

far right
Robert Mitchum (1917–97)
A gorgeous "hunk of guy" with a memorable and distinctive "supermasculine" voice, who was a top star for decades. Never once took his career (or carousing) seriously, though once nominated for an Oscar (1945's *The Story of G. I. Joe*, playing Lt. Walker). Very ba-a-a-d (and that's good) as the sinister lead in *The Night of the Hunter* (1955). Best feature, besides the great build: those sexy "bedroom" eyes. (*Kobal*)

These beefy behemoths were physically and spiritually in opposition to the majority of men who inhabited film before they came along during (and after) World War II. Prior to their invasion, leading men were seen as stylish, somewhat effete, anecdotes to Depression doldrums, and nearly as sensitive and romantic as the females they were courting. So the "he-man" had to *straighten* all that out and let us (and the world) know that the boys were in charge. (Of course, when the majority of them were off playing soldier, women had a field day, in film *and* factories across the country, showing us who was really boss.)

leading Man

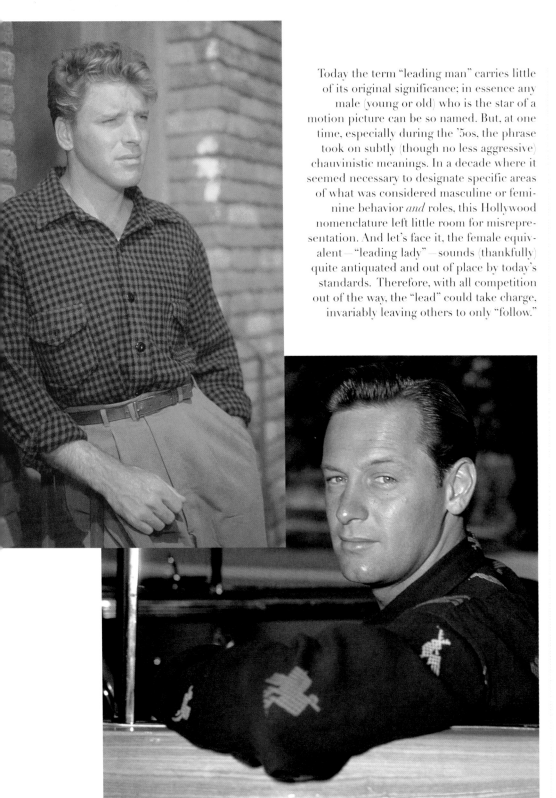

Today the term "leading man" carries little of its original significance; in essence any male (young or old) who is the star of a motion picture can be so named. But, at one time, especially during the '50s, the phrase took on subtly (though no less aggressive) chauvinistic meanings. In a decade where it seemed necessary to designate specific areas of what was considered masculine or feminine behavior *and* roles, this Hollywood nomenclature left little room for misrepresentation. And let's face it, the female equivalent — "leading lady" — sounds (thankfully) quite antiquated and out of place by today's standards. Therefore, with all competition out of the way, the "lead" could take charge, invariably leaving others to only "follow."

from left to right

Kirk Douglas (b. 1916)
A professional wrestler (woof!) who put himself through acting school, Douglas is a paradox of sorts. Playing hard-hitting machismo-types on-screen, he is remarkably charitable off. Never an Oscar winner (except for a 1996 Special Award), he has been nominated thrice. To catch some of that "Greco-Roman" muscle in action, watch *Spartacus* (1960); or if you like 'em in clothes, *The Bad and the Beautiful* (1953). One of the most famous physical features of any star: Douglas's cleft chin (something I once thought you could get with a little adhesive tape and some patience). *(Kobal)*

Burt Lancaster (1913–94)
Inching perilously close to "overacting" in some roles, Lancaster made a career out of "hellfire and brimstone" characters. If you like your acting "larger than life," here is your man. However, his often grandiose mannerisms were well-suited to a number of pictures, among them his Oscar-winner, the title role in *Elmer Gantry* (1960). Matching his talents, though, were his neoclassic looks, making him physically the perfect "leading man." No better example of this is his oceanside love scene with Deborah Kerr in *From Here to Eternity* (1953), where they barely got past the censors. Most infamous item from his past: nude photos of a muscular, young Burt (when he was at his "prettiest") that pop up from time to time. Most interesting physical feature: his hairstyle, which like so many stars then and now, never seemed to change (or get mussed). *(Kobal)*

William Holden (1918–81)
Often slickly, but pleasantly handsome, Holden was the original Hollywood "Golden Boy" in the 1939 screen adaptation of the Odets play and became possibly the most "romantic" lead of the half-dozen or so big male stars of the '50s (which was not *that* hard to do). This by virtue, if for nothing else, of his supersexy (and thankfully) often shirtless role in 1955's *Picnic*, a character that he was first considered too old to play (he was thirty-seven). Beefy *and* beauteous in *Sunset Boulevard* (1950), *Stalag 17* (1953), for which he snagged an Oscar, and *Love Is a Many Splendored Thing* (1955). Great temporary look: as a blond in *Sabrina* (1954). Great permanent feature: his "ski-slope" nose. *(Kobal)*

"Two things will give a man longevity in the public's eye: either classic good looks or an incredible force of personality. The very rare man who combines both is truly memorable."
—*Susan Toepfer*

To be a "man's man" is the highest honor one guy can give to another. It says that in their estimation, you exemplify to the highest degree all the finest masculine characteristics known to mankind and are a shining example to them (and the world) of all that is manly. They are proud to know you and can, without question or hesitation, accept you in their company. From your valorous behavior to refraining from unnecessary shows of emotion, there isn't a single feminine or fey thing about you. They would be proud to call you "friend." But how hard is it to be so iconic and stalwart, and face it, no one is that one-sided. Sadly, unlike the hero who is not so stringently defined, little room is given the "man's man" for *deviation* (though to them the word must sound repellent). Of course, in this day and age, being a "man's man" sounds less and less "honorable" and more like an attempt by some to salvage the last vestiges of outdated and unsympathetic standards from a segregated and stereotyped past. Fortunately, the canniest of these individuals know enough to keep the best of their manly traits, like loyalty, perseverance, and strength of character (although those can be womanly, too), throw out the worst (from sexism to things like leaving the seat down), and incorporate aspects of being conscious of the present and finally, having the humility to care little if they keep the title or not.

Man's Man

"The stereotype used to be that women (because we were unable to do so ourselves) looked for financial support from a mate, and therefore cared less about (his) appearance. But that's not so much the case now, as more and more women can take care of ourselves, giving us the freedom to choose someone for more emotionally satisfying reasons."
—Gloria Steinem

dude

Finally, the walls are beginning to come down, and the delectable dude (precursor to the hunk) is the perfect messenger boy. Mixing elements of both coasts, with high and low style, slang and proper lan-

"A small bit of vanity is not such a bad thing. In fact, I think it's wonderful that we care about the way we look, and try to look attractive to others. Besides, animals (especially males) are well-known to 'primp and fuss' in order to attract the desires of another. So for that matter, it's only natural."
— Geoffrey Beene

guage, Western cowboy with Eastern dandy, the name is given mainly by one male to another (though because of its ambiguous origins, not *necessarily* void of sexual connotations). However, it is more a term of nonphysical endearment and becomes interchangeable with other simple synonyms as guy and fella. Now, isn't that sweet?

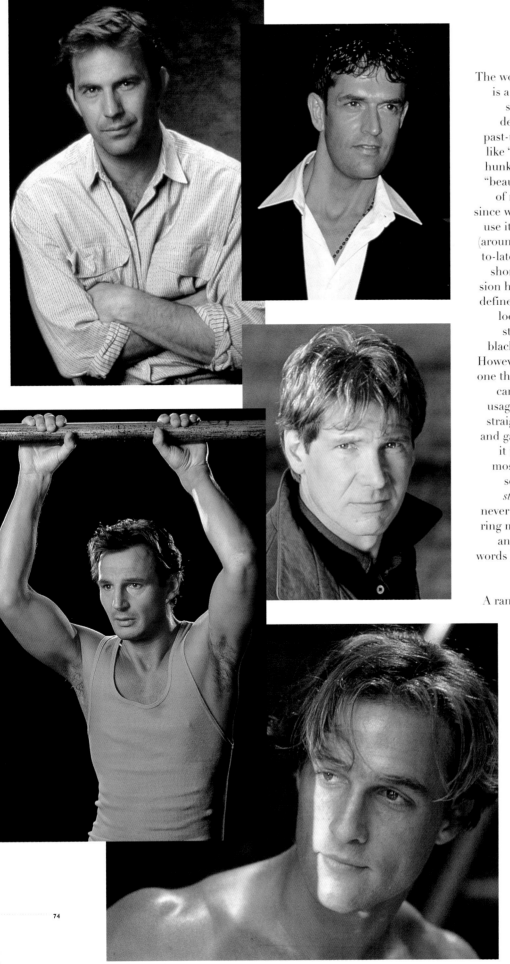

The word "hunk" is a marvelous single word derivation of past-used terms like "wonderful hunk of guy" or "beautiful hunk of man." Ever since we began to use it in earnest (around the mid-to-late '70s), this shortened version has come to define *any* good-looking man: straight, gay, black, or white. However, there is one thing significant about its usage. Whereas straight women and gay men use it to describe most all handsome males, *straight* men never do, preferring more sexual and salacious words like "stud." Hmmm.

A random list of hunks:
Clooney
Gibson
Willis
Quaid
Brosnan
Snipes
Cage
Patric
Pearce
Kilmer
LaPaglia
Roberts
Affleck
Sands
Zane
Bacon
Duchovny
Schaech
Swayze

clockwise, starting from left, top

Kevin Costner (b. 1955)
A major screen force from the late '80s to early '90s, though a bit less so in the last couple of years. Regardless of his recent career shortcomings, this "superstar" is as "hunky" as you can get (without a license), especially so in *The Untouchables* (1987), looking great in a pair of jeans in *Field of Dreams* (1989), and looking quite fetching in tights as the lead in *Robin Hood, Prince of Thieves* (1991). Oscar winner (and buttocks-bearer) as director of *Dances with Wolves* (1990). (Everett Collection)

Rupert Everett (b. 1959)
Whether he is comfortable with the title or not, Everett is *the* cinema's first out-of-the-closet gay male "pin-up" boy. After a bit of career meandering though, with the occasional well-placed landing, as in 1984's gay-fave *Another Country* (originating the role on stage in London) and *Dance with a Stranger* (1985), he was handed the ribbon after his scene-stealing role, as the "very-out-and-Cary-Grantish" boss, in *My Best Friend's Wedding* (1997). (Everett Collection)

Harrison Ford (b. 1942)
If one needed a good example to show how well men age, you wouldn't have to look much further than this guy. Beginning his career in the late '60s, this veritable "heart stopper" has become one of the most successful male leads of all time, with a list of hits that include *American Graffiti* (1973), *Star Wars* (1977), *Raiders of the Lost Ark* (1981), *Blade Runner* (1982), *Presumed Innocent* (1990), *The Fugitive* (1993), and *Air Force One* (1997). (Everett Collection)

Matthew McConaughey (b. 1969)
"Boy toy" as serious actor, and a recent addition to the realm of "matinee idol." Fabulously shirtless in *A Time to Kill* (1996), he played what could be considered the "female" role to Jodie Foster's "male" in the sci-fi pic *Contact* (1997). If we can get beyond the looks (but who'd want to) there might be a good actor underneath all that muscle! (Kobal)

Liam Neeson (b. 1952)
This powerfully built "hulk" of a man has a surprisingly sensitive range as an actor, and in having such becomes the '90s distillation of a work ethic begun with gentlemen like fellow-actor Gregory Peck, with the added bonus of some very nice physical attributes. Oscar nominee as Oskar Schindler in Spielberg's acclaimed *Schindler's List* (1993), he is married to actress Natasha Richardson. (Everett Collection)

far right

Denzel Washington (b. 1954)
Virile, Oscar winner (for 1989's *Glory*) and nominee for *Malcolm X* (1992), Denzel became Tinseltown's first black male "superstar" (an accolade that was too long in coming). Though despite the praise given to supertalent Sidney Poitier (for many years prior), it wasn't until the box-office clout exhibited by a stately Washington, that a man of color could finally command the financial rewards that distinguished "admittance" into such a rarefied group. Once considered being a doctor or journalist, Washington also appeared as a regular on TV's "St. Elsewhere" (from 1982-88). (Everett Collection)

"A male beauty ethic has always existed, it goes back to the most ancient times. However, whether today it's any more real or just a lot of commercial hype is something else."
-- Thomas Hoving

hunk

golden boy

The golden boy, like Midas, can turn everything around him into 24-carat loveliness with a single brush of his hand. He is the hero of Odets's play, bringing redemption and regard to himself and all around him who benefit from his amber glow. The "boy wonder" (or, as some call him, "wonder boy") is the marvelous miracle worker taking the dispirited and giving it life, salvaging the unsalvageable. Seemingly from out of nowhere come these two youths, the most magical males in all of hunkdom, but their place in the sun can be short-lived; like the goose that lays the golden eggs, their stores can run empty, leaving many to seek coin and company with the next just-uncovered gem.

left

Clint Eastwood (b. 1930)
Born during the Depression, Clint has an amazingly long Hollywood career (some four and a half decades), that is marked by many televised and cinematic milestones. The first would be his multiyear run, as Rowdy Yates, in *Rawhide* (1959-66). Not surprisingly, in those early years he was thought of as quite the "pretty boy," despite the unyield character he played. Greater fame was accorded with his notorious "man with no name" incarnation in spaghetti-westerns (so named because they were produced out of Italy), including *A Fistful of Dollars* (1964) and *The Good, The Bad, and The Ugly* (1966). Became a "top" star with his *Dirty Harry* film series, controversially combining sex appeal and brutality. (Audiences ate it up.) Started directing with the "pyscho-killer" flick, *Play Misty For Me* (1971), and gradually, through films like *Bird* (1988), worked his way up to the much-acclaimed Best Picture Oscar winner *The Unforgiven* (1992). Also onetime mayor of Carmel, California (1986-88). Best features: like Paul Newman, all of them, considering too that they've held up so remarkably well over the years. Most forgivable and oddly adorable screen moment: his strained warbling of the Lerner and Loewe ballad, "I Talk to the Trees," from 1969's musical *Paint Your Wagon*. (*Kobal*)

right

Robert Redford (b. 1937)
The blond-haired, blue-eyed, All-American cinematic "ideal" (especially during his mid-'70s popularity stronghold over moviegoers around the world), Redford was so much more than "just another pretty face"—which he proved so eloquently with his astonishing directorial debut, in 1980's *Ordinary People*. As noted now for his environmental-conservation efforts, he is responsible, too, for founding the Sundance Institute (for young filmmakers) which also hosts the United States Film Festival. This "beefy" dude is a giant among movie people. Best on-screen look, while in character (although there are many): in "The Way We Were" (1973). (We can fully appreciate how "Babs" must have felt.) (*Kobal*)

following page

Tom Cruise (b. 1962)
Possibly this generation's one true celluloid "icon." From the moment he so ably slid across the floor in white socks, shirt, and briefs (*sans pantaloons*) in 1983's *Risky Business*, he became the object of desire to millions of women (and men) in darkened theaters across the globe. And though this was not his film debut (that occuring a few years before in *Endless Love*) this slightly "boytoyish" turn immediately gave Cruise a certain attainability that was missing from other stars. He was the perfect blend of "boy-next-door" amiability with "dreamboat" gorgeousness, effortlessly making his way into full-blown "hunkdom" by the end of the decade, with a string of smashes through the '90s establishing him as the screen's "wonder boy." Now looking to branch out into other fields of endeavor, foremostly as producer of his hit thriller, *Mission Impossible* (1996), Tom took over a year off to work with master director Stanley Kubrick for his latest film *Eyes Wide Shut*. Oscar noms for *Born on the Fourth of July* (1989) and *Jerry Maguire* (1996). This onetime high school wrestler's best look: any one where his face shows. (*Everett Collection*)

"I wish there was another word other than 'beauty' to use when describing the attractiveness of some men, because using it suggests a certain amount of vanity, which it does not do when regarding women."
—*Herb Ritts*

boy Wonder

all Singing,
all dancing

Rapture enfolds the hapless hordes with just the sound of his velvet-throated vocals. Swooning, they drift but for mere moments, dreaming he will be theirs forever. He can be manly or he can be mouse, so long as his tones are tender, but mighty is his effect on many a cash register.

left, top
Dean Martin (1917–96, Dino Crocetti)
A onetime prize-fighter, this velvet-voiced *amore* was most famously the singing half to partner Jerry Lewis's comedy half, in one of the most successful collaborations in show-biz history. Beginning in 1946, they lasted through sixteen films, radio, and television, before calling it quits. Martin though, not expected to succeed, managed to do quite well without his rubber-faced friend. Not only an accomplished singer, he conquered (solo) films, concerts, and television (culminating in his long-running self-titled variety series, from 1965-74, featuring the gyrating Golddiggers). Once dubbed "King Leer" by *Life* magazine, for his devilish ways. Biggest music hits: 1955's "Memories Are Made Of This" and "Everybody Loves Somebody," both hitting number one. (*MacFadden/Corbis-Bettmann*)

left, middle
Bing Crosby (1903–77)
"Der Bingle" began singing professionally while still in college, made his film debut in 1930, and signed on to host his own radio show shortly thereafter. Almost immediately he began selling records (in the millions), ending up as one of the most successful entertainers (creatively *and* financially) of all time. Throughout his almost five-decade career he became a "father figure" to countless families across America and the world, although his own family life was far from idyllic (among other things, for all his wealth, he was notoriously tight with money). Nevertheless, Bing gave the world much in the way of grand entertainment, not the least of them his rendition of the holiday standard "White Christmas," which he introduced in his 1942 film, *Holiday Inn*. (It was also the biggest-selling single of all time until it was surpassed by Elton John's Princess Diana tribute, "Candle In The Wind, 1997.") As famous for his love of golf (and orange juice), Crosby also won the Oscar for *Going My Way* (1944). (*Kobal*)

left, bottom
Perry Como (b. 1912)
With his relaxed (at times seemingly lethargic) delivery, Como left listeners spellbound to the tune of dozens of top-10 hits. A barber before he was a singer, Como also went on to accumulate three Emmys, two Peabodys, and a Grammy. Once, too, the highest-paid entertainer of all time. One of his most melodious moments: "Catch a Falling Star" (1958). (*Corbis-Bettmann*)

right
Frank Sinatra (1915–98)
Whether he's referred to as "Ole Blue Eyes," "Chairman of the Board," or "The Voice" there's no mistaking the gentleman himself, but fame on this level does not come without hardship, struggle, and controversy, and Sinatra's life had plenty of it. From his humble beginnings in Hoboken, New Jersey, to the (temporary) loss of his singing voice in 1952 (which, at the time, ended his long-term recording contract), to the machinations of his acting career, and scandal surrounding his much-reported underworld connections, Sinatra's whole professional life was one of true celebrity. An Oscar (for 1953's *From Here to Eternity*), multi Grammy (including three for "Album of the Year") and Medal of Freedom winner, an often "brutish" Sinatra began as the "idol" of countless female bobby-soxers and ended it as (arguably) the most popular singer of all time. A quintessential Sinatra tune: "Strangers in the Night," a 1966 number-one hit from the film, *A Man Could Get Killed*. (*Michael Ochs Archives*)

Crooner

Music Man

"Music doth soothe the savage breast," so the saying goes. Even the surliest among us cannot help but be moved by the beat of a big band, running to the dance floor with our two left feet; or surrender to a symphony, and find emotion in remaining motionless. And only a cad could scowl at a piano player, plunking out tune after tune on his ebony- and ivory-sheathed instrument. And every once in a while, one of these men becomes as famed as his fanfare, and people flock to see what all the noise is about.

far left
Leonard Bernstein (1919–90)
Wickedly handsome, no doubt considered even more so because of the "passionate" nature of his profession, Bernstein led the New York Philharmonic from 1957 to 1970, though beyond Manhattan's shores he is probably most widely remembered as the composer of *Candide*, *On The Town*, and especially, *West Side Story*. Won two Emmys with the Philharmonic, during the '60s. (*National Archives/Corbis-Bettmann*)

near left, top
Harry James (b. 1916)
Though not necessarily attractive in the classical sense, Harry had a charismatic way about him that was absolutely irresistible to woman. Perhaps his sensational handling of the trumpet, while fronting his own band, added to the allure. Whatever the reasons were, James managed a coup by wedding (then) America's favorite "pin-up girl," Betty Grable. Once a member of Benny Goodman's orchestra, this son of a circus bandleader also appeared in a number of films, including *Springtime in the Rockies* and *Two Girls and a Sailor*. (*Kobal*)

near left, bottom
Liberace
(1919–87. Wladziu Valentino Liberace)
Every mother's favorite piano player, Liberace made a hugely successful career out of highly competent "tickling of the ivories" and flaunting his wealth in the most audacious ways imaginable. Surrounding himself with signature regalia (besequined clothes, jewel-encrusted sets, etc) and "I love mom best" repartee amazingly endeared him to his fans, of which there were many more than you could have imagined. Later years and death were marred by scandal involving his personal life. Most famous accoutrement: his candelabras. Famous saying, when his music was criticized: that he and his workers would, "cry all the way to the bank." (*Michael Ochs Archives*)

Singers and musicians are cast in roles just like their silver-screen counterparts. They are given a part to play and a specific audience to please. They also suffer from typecasting, repetitive product, over-hyping, and watching their audiences outgrow them. However, forgetting appearances, music has long been the more intimate of the two. Way before we had home invaders like video, computers, and the Internet, and with going to a film an experience we shared with others (family and strangers), music, for the longest time, wafted unabated through every private household. But this intrusion did not go on without dispute, and for that reason melody-makers have always suffered from a type of musical polarization. For every member of the older generation contending with the evils of the newest music craze from jazz, swing, be-bop, and rock 'n' roll, to disco, hip-hop and rap, their children stood ground on the opposite side. And these divisions occurred not only along familial lines, but political and social ones, too. While indoor neighbor television remained neutral and family-oriented, music formats (hopefully without deliberate intention) segregated adults from teenagers, country music lovers from worshippers of soul, with only the occasional poorly programmed Top-40 station thrown in for good measure. Oddly enough, even within each category of music there would be a division between young and old, good and bad, better and worse, and for each separation there would be a poster boy (or girl) extolling the virtues of their particular parcel. However, time usually wins out over all, and one era's musical rebel becomes this epoch's nostalgic emblem of yesterday's hottest hits.

"Men are being looked at more and more as objects, and less and less as the personification of an ideal."
— Susan Toepfer

left
Pat Boone (b. 1934)
Though not done deliberately so, Boone's existence seemed solely invented to counteract the "dangers" of rock 'n' roll, or, more specifically, to assuage listeners away from singers like Elvis Presley. But true or not, Boone's resulting immense popularity clearly indicated that he (at least) partially *accomplished* the task. A Columbia grad (magna cum laude), this warbling "boy-next-door" had some measured success in films, too. Though for all his devout Christianity, Hollywood seemed an odd place for him to be. Biggest music hits, among many: "April Love" from the film (in which he starred) of the same name, and "Love Letters in the Sand," both from 1957. Most amazing discovery: with the religious bluster notwithstanding, he really was very cute and the white bucks were always a nice touch. Most telling professional development: his recent release of a "heavy-metal" inspired album, much to the chagrin and dismay of many long-time fans. What was he thinking? (*MacFadden/Corbis-Bettmann*)

above
Elvis Presley (1935–77)
With hundreds of biographies in print, Elvis's humble beginnings in Tupelo, Mississippi, and Memphis, Tennessee, are presumably well-known to the public. Which leaves necessary only a brief recounting of some notable pieces of his life, then and thereafter. Elvis was the surviving sibling of identical twins; his house also being spared from a devastating tornado when he was only one year old. He earned the nickname "Elvis the Pelvis" for the provocative modulations and gyrations of his hips while performing; causing him to be shot from above the waist during his famous visit on "The Ed Sullivan Show." He appeared in over thirty-three films; none were critical successes though most were financially rewarding. Sold over six-hundred million records, a possible record for a single artist; won only a Lifetime Achievement Grammy in 1971. A kind and generous man; felt by many instrumental in the degradation of the youth of his generation. The musical *Bye Bye Birdie* is said to be loosely based on his induction into the army; had a hugely successful stamp made in his honor (a first for a "rock 'n' roller"). Most sensual feature: his "pouty" lips; the fullest this side of Barbara Hershey. (*Graphic House/Corbis-Bettmann*)

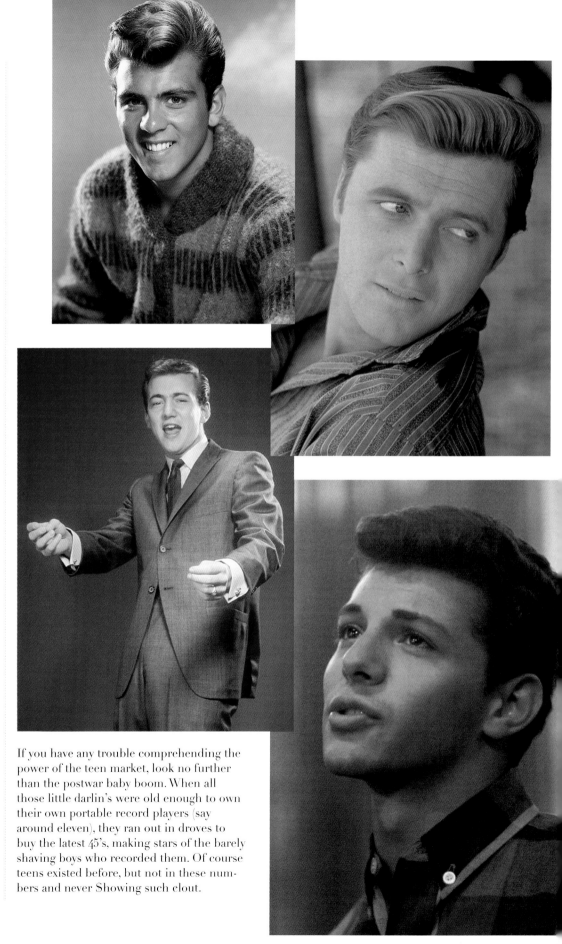

Fabian (b. 1943, Fabian Forte)
One of the first recording stars to go professionally by one name (though he added Forte back in in 1970), Fabian was adorable with a capital "A" starting at the ripe old age of fourteen. Part of a boatload of male teenybopper idols that dotted the landscape of the mid-to-late '50s, this brown-haired, blue-eyed "plaything" tried extending his range by working on films, though it is questionable whether it helped his career or not (with movies came an abrupt end to the success of his records). Biggest hit: "Tiger" in 1959. (*Kobal*)

Edd "Cookie" Byrnes (b. 1933)
Edd caused a sensation among female viewers with his part (as parking lot attendant) in the television series "77 Sunset Strip," forcing producers to expand his minor role to that of featured player. It also resulted in the hit recording of the song "Kookie, Kookie (Lend Me Your Comb)" and a Grammy nomination for Best New Artist. Though his stay at the "top" would be short-lived, the awareness of the power of the teenage consumer would stay with us indefinitely. (*MacFadden/Corbis-Bettmann*)

Bobby Darin
(1936–73, Robert Walden Cassotto) Near-legendary "bad boy" singer and actor (of note). Darin began his too-short life as the son of a single mother (losing his father before birth) and existing on welfare. By the late '50s, though, through a remarkable gift for vocal delivery, emerged as a very popular nightclub and recording star. His version of "Mack the Knife" in 1959 won him two Grammys (for Record of the Year and Best New Artist). Sexy *and* vulnerable, he was the perfect antithesis to first wife, actress Sandra Dee (of *Gidget* fame). Captured an Oscar nomination for his work in *Captain Newman, M.D.* (1963). Died after an operation at thirty-seven, heart trouble having plagued him his whole life. 1990 Rock and Roll Hall of Famer. (*MacFadden/Corbis-Bettmann*)

Frankie Avalon (b. 1939)
Responsible for the smash "Venus," Avalon was a musical prodigy (with the trumpet at the age of nine) and movie star by the late '50s. Notable for his *Beach Party* film series with Annette Funicello, this perpetual teenager (never growing old like Dick Clark) continues working today. Once managed by the same individual who discovered Fabian, Bob Marcucci. A couple films of note: *The Alamo* (1960) and *Voyage to the Bottom of the Sea* (1961). Visual trademarks: the impenetrable hairstyle and square-cut swim trunks (to Annette's one-piece). (*MacFadden/Corbis-Bettmann*)

Tommy Sands (b. 1937)
This "stud-puppy" was already on television by the time he was eleven and had a top-ten music hit (the anthemic "Teen-Age Crush") by age twenty, before graduating to films in 1958. Once the son-in-law of Frank Sinatra (married to daughter Nancy from 1960-65), Sands balanced a career as teen-to-young-adult "heartthrob" until illness forced a temporary halt to work. Appeared in *Babes in Toyland* (1961) and *The Longest Day* (1962). (*Graphic House/Corbis-Bettmann*)

"Beauty (male or female) is agreeable to the eye and good for the spirit."
–Douglas Fairbanks, Jr.

If you have any trouble comprehending the power of the teen market, look no further than the postwar baby boom. When all those little darlin's were old enough to own their own portable record players (say around eleven), they ran out in droves to buy the latest 45's, making stars of the barely shaving boys who recorded them. Of course teens existed before, but not in these numbers and never showing such clout.

teen idol

near and far right:
Ricky Nelson (1940–85) and **David Nelson** (b.1936)
That television's real-life couple Ozzie and Harriet (of "The Adventures of Ozzie and Harriet") could have two so gorgeous boys, did wonders for the success of their long-running series. An ever-adoring (young female) public could pick her favorite: either blond or brown-haired, good or (never-too) bad, thin or stocky. Ricky quickly became one of the first true "teen idols" of the rock era, growing from cute "pretty boy" adolescent to magnificently handsome young man on small screens throughout the country. And while on his journey, he amassed an enormous string of top-40 hits, including "Poor Little Fool" and "Traveling Man," culminating in induction into the Rock and Roll Hall of Fame (awarded posthumously, 1987). David, the adorable "boy-next-door" bookend to "randy" Rick, was more laid-back (privately and professionally), and opted to become a television producer and director. Appearing only occasionally before the camera (with the exception of the familial series), cherubic David did have a tasty role in 1957's sensational "Peyton Place." Best physical features: that you could find these "babes" in one household. One-stop shopping. P.S.: dig both boy's "crazy" shoes! (*MacFadden/Corbis-Bettmann*)

"I think a pretty face is more of an obstacle than an invitation."
— Isaac Mizrahi

The lure of sexy siblings is almost too tempting for words. But show business has always understood the attraction, and whenever and wherever it was possible, made next-of-kin available to the buying public. I mean, if you can get two (or, God help us, more) for the price of one, what would you do? And being that it's pretty uncommon to have more than one substantial "cutie-pie" per family (unless you're a Baldwin or a Kennedy) to give your attention to, savor the moment if you find yourself vexed with such a decision.

for ladies 0nly

In an era defined by the "idols" of teenagers of the late '50s and early '60s, mothers were not going to let their daughters have *all* the fun. As juveniles they were weaned on the melodious incantations of Sinatra, Crosby, Como, and Martin; now maturer as women, possibly a bit grayer of hair, they were still none the less romantic and musically inclined. Thus was born the unknowingly suggestive category of "adult contemporary" music (and what to some belongs in an elevator). However, into this realm fall such greats (and near-greats) as Andy Williams, Bobby Vinton, Engelbert Humperdinck, Jack Jones, through James Taylor, Gilbert O'Sullivan, and into recent Rod Stewart and Elton John vinyls. Though created to differentiate between and keep separate "kids" and "grown-up" consumers, nevertheless, it is the rare (young) person who can withstand the libidinous allure of such "seasoned" music; conversely, what (older) person cannot admit to the attraction of pulsating pubescence.

left
Robert Goulet (b. 1933)
The best-looking thing to hit Broadway since colored lights. This harmonic "hunk" was one of the last of "The Great White Way" sensations, in an era when stars were still being born overnight. A smash with his stage debut (as Sir Lancelot) in *Camelot* (1960), Goulet quickly went on to success in concerts, television, film, and recording. A Grammy winner in 1962 for Best New Artist and Tony winner for *The Happy Time* (1968). (*MPTV Archives*)

right
Tom Jones (b. 1940)
Every mother's secret music "fantasy" mate, or so it would appear. Girls didn't like him, but women did, in droves. The AC (adult contemporary) equivalent to Elvis Presley, with much the same pelvic activity. A Best New Artist Grammy winner in 1965, this lustfully lyric "lad" from South Wales was a concert-ticket-selling bonanza, supposedly not losing much of his popularity even today. A couple of his biggest hits: "What's New Pussycat?" (1965) and "She's a Lady" (1971). Biggest lost marketing opportunity: selling his sweat to hordes of screaming ladies. (*Everett Collection*)

"Asking women what they think about beautiful men is potent; it is impossible for them to answer without feeling some emotion based on how they themselves were treated for their looks, either as an individual or as a sex."
— *Linda Wells*

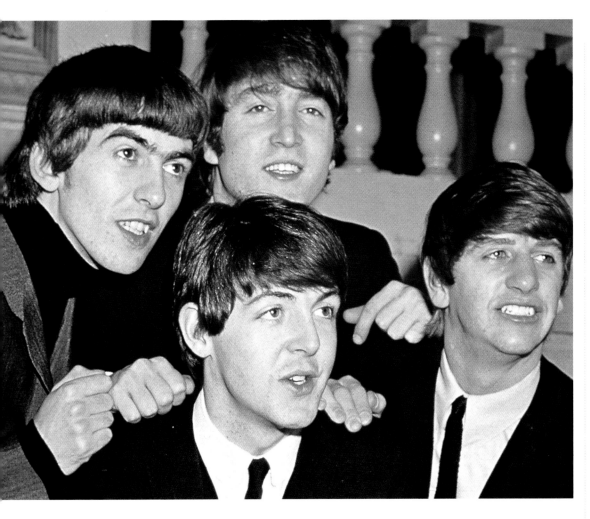

Aside from the obvious benefits of having all your musical bases covered (a keyboardist, bass player, lead vocalist, and so on), a group of guys gives the *fans* so much more to work with, and we are the ones who must be pleased. The law of averages says you can always find something you like if given enough choice, right? So this point is not lost on quartets and quintets, even though they would be the last to admit any of their ranks was chosen on looks as much as talent. Of course, the existence of such recent gorgeous gatherings as the Backstreet Boys, and, even more famously, the New Kids on the Block and Menudo, seems to suggest less a lottery of getting whatever comes in the door with guitar-in-hand, than a deliberate attempt to find the most devastating dude around who can still carry a tune.

"Some women now look at men as a 'piece of meat,' our description of how they have always appraised us; other women, hopefully, bring to voyeurism a natural talent, along with a memory, of how we always wished men would see us."
—*Nancy Friday, from her book,* The Power of Beauty

boys in the band

This category belongs not only to every younger or older sister, but to *anyone* who ever had a secret crush on a cute boy singer. Those teenage years would have been unbearable without the fantasy romances they made possible. Singing every song especially for you (and only you), they made youthful heartache a pleasant passage.

"Things always change, fifteen years ago who would have thought body piercing would be so popular? What's coming next? We're probably going to be attracted to what we're not attracted to now, but I don't think we'll ever find bad breath attractive."
— Helen Gurley Brown

far left
Donny Osmond (b. 1957)
Every sister's girlhood crush. Like Michael (from The Jackson 5), it was evident that Donny supplied all the heat for the Osmond Brothers. After dropping the smarmy childhood sweetness of his years featured on "The Andy Williams Show," Donny quickly grew into the musical "boy toy" of the second-coming of teen male "heartthrobs." Though a little too saccharin for some, Donny-boy did exude a certain sex appeal that was undeniable, even to his most vocal opponents. And in a subtle visual twist, deliberate or not, was allowed to spotlight his mighty fine posterior (on his hit variety series, "Donny and Marie"), whereas sister-dear never bared an inch of cleavage. Best asset: aside from the obvious pun, a Pepsodent smile. (*Michael Ochs Archives*)

left, top
Andy Gibb (1958–88)
Certainly more sexual than his contemporaries (like Mssrs. Osmond, Manilow, and Jackson), Gibb still appealed to many of the same fans (if for more covert reasons). With the shadow of his famous brothers conveniently moved aside for the time being, Gibb was thrust into the forefront by a string of late '70s global smashes, that included "I Just Want To Be Your Everything," "(Love Is) Thicker Than Water," and "Shadow Dancing." However, all his fame and riches could not make him happy and for his whole short adult life had to deal with substance abuse, before succumbing to death by heart inflammation. Favored performing look: shirtless, and supertight pants. Do I see a problem, here? I think not. (*Michael Ochs Archives*)

left, middle
Barry Manilow (b. 1946, Barry Alan Pincus)
Manilow is something of an anomaly, far from drop-dead gorgeous and more or less lacking in typical sex appeal, he (at one time) literally had to beat off the fans with a stick. It says a lot about the power of (his) music, that a gawky, awkward "jingle" writer could seemingly so easily reach the top of his game. Also one of the rare singers who topped both the Hot 100 and Adult Contemporary charts, simultaneously. Infamously starting out as an accompanist for Bette Midler at The Continental Baths (in New York), Barry first scored big with his number-one cover of "Mandy" in 1974. Subsequent ditties from this toothy tunesmith include, "I Write the Songs" and "Copacabana." Wrote McDonald's "You Deserve A Break Today." Best physical feature: if you like noses, he's your man. (*Everett Collection*)

left, bottom
Michael Jackson (b. 1958)
Somewhere in the middle between adorable adolescent and surreal adult there lay quite the young "hunk." Arguably, around the time he released his "Off the Wall" album, Michael was setting hearts aflutter and began (in earnest) to send cash registers a-ringing. Famously discovered, along with his brothers, by Miss Diana Ross, he quickly stole the spotlight away from his unawares siblings. By the release of the smasheroo-album "Thriller" though, slight signs of egomania were showing. Then, once he proclaimed himself "The King of Pop" all connections to his former physical and spiritual self were severed. Regardless, ditties like "Rock with You" abound (alongside their pleasantly under-produced video-counterparts), with all their innocent charm and attraction intact. Grammy Living Legend in 1993. (*Michael Ochs Archives*)

near right, top

Paul "Bono" Hewson (b. 1960)
Lead vocalist of the Irish rock band U2. Following in the footsteps of other famed frontmen (Mick Jagger, Roger Daltrey, Van Morrison, et. al.), Bono is the perfect physical evolution of his predecessors. And taking full advantage of groundwork they laid, Bono is able to appeal openly to women and both straight and gay males, losing nothing in the transaction (more likely gaining something). However, it is the ambiguity surrounding his sexual attractiveness that says as much about the open-mindedness of his fans, as it does about the undeniable handsomeness of the man himself. Plaintively wailing in the hit, "I Still Haven't Found What I'm Looking For," this married man with two kids looks fantastic in anything tight and black. Best for his black wraparound sunglasses. Original full nickname "bono-vox" was the name of a neighborhood store; Latin for "perfect-voice." (*Lisa Haun/Michael Ochs Archives*)

near right, middle

Vanilla Ice (b. 1968, Robert Van Winkle)
We all hate to admit it, but Mr. Ice was one handsome dude, so delectable in fact that he could have been a model (which he was in Madonna's book, *Sex*). Mr. "Square-Jaw" was also one in a string of media-hyped "one-hit wonders" (in this case, two) that have punctuated the music scene since the advent of recorded sound. Some of his recent comely compadres include Gerardo, Snow, and Tommy Page. (*Everett Collection*)

middle right, middle

George Michael
(b. 1963, Georgios Kyriacos Panayiotou)
In the beginning, Georgie-Porgie was almost too pretty (to the point of feminine) for all the tousled and highlighted hair, dark lashes, and pearly whites. Not that his fans seemed to mind. And in an age where gender was less a factor, those numbered almost equally among young girls *and* boys. His early '80s pairing (as Wham!) with equally babalicious (though not as talented) Andrew Ridgely was a sensation until George (and rightly so) took over the spotlight. As a solo act, Michael trimmed the hair, added stubble, and donned tight jeans, to the enamor of already devoted followers. With openly provocative hits like "I Want Your Sex" he pushed further out on the edge of pop music than many of his peers, only to fall off himself in the midst of a late '90s sex scandal. Most important influence on the way guys wanted to look: with he and Don Johnson, made not shaving the sexiest and simplest male fashion trend of the '80s. (*Everett Collection*)

middle right, bottom

The Artist (formerly known as Prince)
(b. 1958, Prince Roger Nelson)
If sexual ambiguity is your thing, then The Artist is your "man." At times openly courting controversy, Mr. Nelson relished in the brouhaha (that surrounded his personal and professional life) and has stayed a major force in music despite less-than-stellar sales in recent years. From his first top-20 hit "I Wanna Be Your Lover" his signature percussive and rhythmic tracks were evident, as were his soon-to-be-familiar sexually teasing lyrics, though his early dance smash "Controversy" may be a better indicator. A dynamic onstage performer, he has penned almost as many hits for others ("Nothing Compares to U" and "Manic Monday" as two examples), as he has for himself. Oscar winner (for song score) for 1984's *Purple Rain*. His dapper dressing style is a good argument for men wearing heels. Best display of his tight Napoleonic body: in the video for "Kiss" (1986). (*Everett Collection*)

far right

Rick Springfield (b. 1949)
As a top "rocker" Rick's fame may be questionable, as a "heartthrob" however, there is little dispute. Skinny, and a bit too boyish, Springfield took the looks God gave him and made the most of them—though as Dr. Noah Drake (on the soap opera "General Hospital"), his pampered puss may have been more at home. For a year was a singing cartoon character in "Mission Magic" (1974). Biggest music hit: 1981's "Jesse's Girl" (for which he won the Grammy). (*Everett Collection*)

> "Many of us are such victims of what is dictated through popular culture that we will be convinced it is alluring if *Allure* magazine tells us it is."
> —*Michelangelo Signorile*

By the time the '80s were ending and the '90s came around, a lot of the *innocence* in music (and much of life in general) had been lost or was fast fading away. But many of the things we got in place of it, while different, may be just as good. Musically, this meant a greater acceptance and understanding of diversity. It also allowed that we could have more ambiguous musical "idols," philosophically, spiritually, and sexually, which in turn opened up new markets that better served these newly discovered consumers. So from Sting to Jon B., Corey Hart to Ricky Martin, from a time that saw the death of disco to its rebirth, music has never been more mixed, nor are its men more attractive.

97

Bruce Springsteen (b. 1949)
left
Bruce Springsteen (b. 1949)
Hubba-hubba! For a spell there, the absolute sexiest rock singer in the universe. Whoever convinced him to pump iron should be congratulated. How could you take your eyes off those biceps! Obviously very few could, though his fame began well before perfecting those pecs. Starting in 1975 (with "Born to Run"), through "Hungry Heart" in 1980 and "Dancing in the Dark" (1984), Brucie-boy was the magnificent manifestation of manly motion, and oh-so American, too. Despite a slowdown in the late '80s and early '90s, came back a little disheveled (though only infinitesimally less attractive for it) and ever more endearing for his fantastic penning and performance of "Streets of Philadelphia," his 1994 Oscar-winning song for the film *Philadelphia.* Best look: if you have to ask, you aren't paying attention. *(Richard McCaffrey/Michael Ochs Archives)*

right
Garth Brooks (b. 1962)
Coming in on the heels of other down-home "hunks," this husky 6' high school jock did more for country music than just sell records (which he does to an unbelievable degree); he revolutionized it. Writing about prescient themes, like battery and homosexuality, this "teddy-bear" singer-guitarist strummed his way to the top of *both* the country and pop charts, and in the process sold faster than any other recording artist in history. Ironically, he has never had a hit single crack the "Hot 100." Also proof that you don't have to look like a body-builder to woo fans. Besides, there's more of him to love. *(Ron Wolfson/Michael Ochs Archives)*

With time comes understanding and, we hope, acceptance. So it seems that, after all the shouting and brouhaha about how bad this guy was and how he should stay away from your daughters and all that music's just noise, the "rocker" has finally become America's favorite son. (Under the right circumstances, you can add sexiest, too.)

Country boys have always been kinda' cute, I mean who could resist Gene Pitney or Glen Campbell. But it wasn't until they got hold of some barbells, that these "good 'ole boys" started giving off some real heat. I recollect Randy Travis as the first to add real "muscle" to his music, ably accompanied by, among others, Clint Black, Aaron Tippen, Ricky Van Shelton, George Strait, and who can forget, Billy Ray Cyrus (although, what is up with that hair?). For their efforts, the genre has never been more popular, proving that sex (especially if it wears a ten-gallon hat and *little* else) sells.

"To a certain extent we are being desensitized by all these male images. Straight and gay men can both be attracted to them, groups that are normally very suspicious of one another. Now we're seeing that despite the differences we have as men, we have a lot of similarities in what attracts us."
—Michael Lafavore

A song's emotional impact can be so immediate (it has to be with tunes lasting no more than a few minutes) that it's easy to get caught up. Whether they are simple melodies or compositions of unbelievable intricacy they can effect feelings of great joy, immense sorrow, and overwhelming passion. Regardless of how we are swayed, these miracles of melody can inspire entire populations to stand up and cheer, or one individual to lay down and weep.

left
Kurt Cobain (1967–94)
Lead singer of the "grunge" group Nirvana, and fair-haired figurehead in a smallish, but noisy music revolution. Mixing rock with ample doses of despair, dissolution (and the occasional frock dress), Cobain's band Nirvana and other groups like Pearl Jam left their Pacific Northwest homes and set out to "sensitize" Generation-Xers. Winsomely handsome, Cobain surrendered to his own demons by taking his own life in 1994, leaving millions of dollars and a grieving wife, Courtney Love–who once tellingly said of Kurt, "it was like being married to a gay man." She meant it in the nicest way. Reaction to his good looks: made you want to hug him. (Joe Hughes/Michael Ochs Archives)

right]
Babyface (b. 1959, Kenneth Edmonds)
This debonair songster is as welcome behind the scenes as he is in front of the mike. Multi-Grammy-winner, sometimes along with partner LA Reid, Babyface is responsible for the hits of many other artists, including Whitney Houston and Toni Braxton. Irresistible to fans, his cool, effortless style recalls that of past musical giants. Nat King Cole and Sam Cooke, updated with a '90s sensuality and sensibility. (photo courtesy of Rocky Schenk)

"Today we have a broader spectrum of beauty images in terms of racial diversity, but we still follow more or less the same physical guidelines —symmetry, a great nose, eyes, mouth— when it comes to the individual and what makes him attractive."
—Susan Toepfer

agony & ecstasy

"Surprisingly, male stars were once much more androgynous than they are today—they wore obvious makeup, they were elegant, sensitive, romantic, and graceful. They were gentlemen, not beefcake. Leslie Howard, Valentino, William Powell, Fred Astaire cannot exist in a world that polarizes gay and straight identities."
—Amy Fine Collins

Graceful, sophisticated, and agile—these are just a few of the words that can describe the "hoofer," though the word itself sounds rather clumsily endearing for someone who can tread so softly before the footlights. For a time, these lovable lopers were everywhere, but now not nearly as plentiful. Falling victim to our seemingly dreamless times, they'd be nonexistent if it weren't for the occasional music video or Broadway show.

hoofer

Song & dance

"The physical is entirely mutable; if someone's character is attractive they become attractive physically. Whereas, if their personality is not engaging, no amount of looks can save them."
—Linda Wells

No one is more adorable than a song and dance man, a fella' who took the obvious attractions of both dancing and singing, mellowed things a bit, and came up with a winning combination. Though to find one today is a little like looking for good hard candy at a health food store; they seem a bit too sugary-sweet in our reality-driven times. But in their heyday, with gents like Dan Dailey, they were an unavoidably appealing group of guys.

"I am convinced that by the next century men are going to be 'peacocks'—in higher heels, fancier clothes, and even more makeup than women. Which I think has a lot to do with females being tired and bored with caring about the way they look, and men discovering how much fun it can be."
— *Isaac Mizrahi*

Sometimes the more exotic the better; from ballet to flamenco, tango to two-stepping. And given all the right elements—great music, great costumes, and a great body (from years of physical devotion to your art)—nothing is sexier on two feet. And forget all that sissy stuff you've heard about dancing, when one of these gorgeous guys (straight or gay) waltzes across the floor, you know who's taking the lead.

As nice as the thought is, the beautiful male bodies we worship today are creations of very recent circumstances. In fact, today's magnificently muscled men, like their slightly softer brothers before them, are a reflection of the times in which they live. In this way they are not unlike women's hemlines — considered by some as a barometer of societal and economic standards. In the early part of this century the sight of excessive male flesh (female, too) was frowned upon, so the need to work out and develop a manly physique was basically moot. Who was going to see it? Not surprisingly, as a country, we were isolationist and nonaggressive. By the '20s, public morals had loosened up somewhat, as did clothing and the ways in which our skin was seen.

A nice example are those marvelous men's cut-out bathing suits favored at the time. (Interestingly, this happened after WW I and it would not be the first time popular culture was affected by the sudden reintroduction of thousands of single men back into the mainstream. Thus the sentiment at the time, "how you gonna keep 'em down on the farm, after they've seen Paree!?") During the '30s, with the Depression casting a pall over the entire country, any displays of frivolity were frowned upon. And that included excessive flashes of flesh.

However, those were years of great advances in filmmaking and photography, with the latter benefitting so ably from the male nude as a subject. Then WW II hit, and all the men went overseas, again. And what do countless numbers of men do when they are stuck together (without women) for years at a time? Well there are lots of answers to this question, but in context, a lot of them "pumped iron." So a bodybuilding ethic that had slowly begun before the war, with purveyors like Charles Atlas, found a ready and able home. When the war was over, these healthy lads brought all that brawn back home and continued working out. (Figuring, once you've seen how *beautiful* your body could become, it was hard to stop.) Suddenly the male form was taking real shape and the true "Golden Age" of bodybuilding was born.

From the mid-'40s, gyms across the country pumped out one beefy male

three magnificent men from the "Golden Age" of bodybuilding

left, top
Bud Counts
Was urged by his parents to get into physique modeling to earn back money to pay for all his years of gym training. He was successful and a genre favorite. (Author's collection)

left, bottom
Vic Seipke
This Midwestern hulk was only 5' 9" but packed a wallop when it came to the looks department. Winner of the Mr. America title in 1955. (Author's collection)

right
Ed Fury
Born Ed Holovchik, was along with Steve Reeves, the two most famous and best-looking bodybuilders of the sport's "Golden Age." Though both made attempts at film, Reeves was the more successful, with his Italian *Hercules* series. Nevertheless, Fury was absolutely breathtaking in front of the still camera and his sublime physique is a prime example of the how beautiful a man's body could get by working out naturally. (Author's collection)

"There were two profound influences on the way gay men saw and changed their bodies. The first was AIDS. We felt that having a great, muscular body was a sign that you were healthy (whether this was the case or not). The second was (gay) pornography, which became, during the '80s, the most visible representation our community had of what we looked like (although that physical ideal was often exaggerated). Now, of course, the bodies we developed have carried over into the (straight) mainstream."
— *Michelangelo Signorile*

the physique

much for homo- *and* heterosexuals. Gay men were finding an outlet for their libidos and straight men were finding it hard to admit it was effecting theirs. So not surprisingly, physique poseurs began to head underground, to wait in keep. This left standard bodybuilding to reassert its manly intentions. By the late '50s, many of the younger actors began working out in earnest, compelled on by their attractiveness to an ever-growing youth market. This call-to-arms, so to speak, was not lost on more established stars, either, forcing the domineering, barrel-shaped chests of Victor Mature-types to give way to the lean, hard pectorals of the Paul Newmans. However, all this newly minted muscle would not go on to conquer Hollywood alone, without a good fight; true manliness reasserted itself with the hairy muscularity of men like Sean Connery and Hugh O'Brian (albeit in an even more toned and streamlined version than before). So these titans battled it out throughout the '60s, with the younger set preferring the shaped and shiny, and the older gravitating to the hirsute and husky.

By the end of the '60s with the youth, women's, and gay movements, men really began to change physically (not to mention spiritually). "Flower power" allowed men to

specimen after another. Now, what this did to the country "at-large" was not insignificant. You must remember that prior to the war working out was not what real men did. It was thought of as vain and somewhat feminine to care what "shape" your body was in. Not that health wasn't an issue. Just that laboring over your muscles was too close to beautification. However, the war changed that by showing guys how relatively easy it was to gain muscle mass. You also got bigger, and bigger for any guy was definitely better. Meanwhile back in Hollywood, the well-dressed types of the '30s were fast being replaced by the "he-men" of the '40s. These beasts were a sort of American propaganda move to prove how much stronger we were than the enemy. By the '50s then, men and women (in the movies, especially) were learning to look exactly how they were supposed to: guys being taller, larger, and handsome; women shorter, smaller, and pretty. However, what happens next is more subversive. All those guys working out and proudly showing their wares proved too

"There is nothing good about being treated like an 'object,' human beings are not things. However, equally sharing the insult with men is better than leaving women to deal with it alone. Shit equally divided is better than shit unequally divided."
— *Gloria Steinem*

look androgynous for the first time. With the women's movement it was imperative that men could be *seen* by females. The recognition of a gay faction in our population uncovered the simple truth that *all* men must recognize attraction in and of themselves. So, by the mid-'70s we had beautifully aggressive *and* nonaggressive men, with bodies to match. We soon had a democratic president and times were loose and free. For some, too loose, so by the '80s in came

"I don't really give a damn what a man looks like; the most important thing is that he likes me. Sure, if you delivered George Clooney or Antonio Banderas on a blind date I might think that was pretty dazzling, but if he didn't think I was attractive, he wouldn't be interesting. Why want someone who doesn't want you?"
—*Helen Gurley Brown*

Reagan and the "new" Hollywood supermen, like Schwarzenegger, to take back their rightful place of male superiority and dominance. However, the gains made by women and gay men would not go back in the closet. So this new male body (aided by steroids and Nautilus equipment) began, unwittingly, to walk a thin line between hard-line conservatism and sexism, and "all-access" liberalism. By the end of the decade, while the body stayed hard, the exact definition of his appeal and who, specifically, he was appealing to, blurred almost completely, with a curious footnote: For the past few years, gay men and straight women, plus any other aficionados of pop culture, have favored the slick, newly shaven, "six-pack" carrying, tan-lined, muscle boy, recalling Greek statues. But, as of late, these idolized icons seem to be growing back on some of the hair of the "dog" that bit them. What goes around…

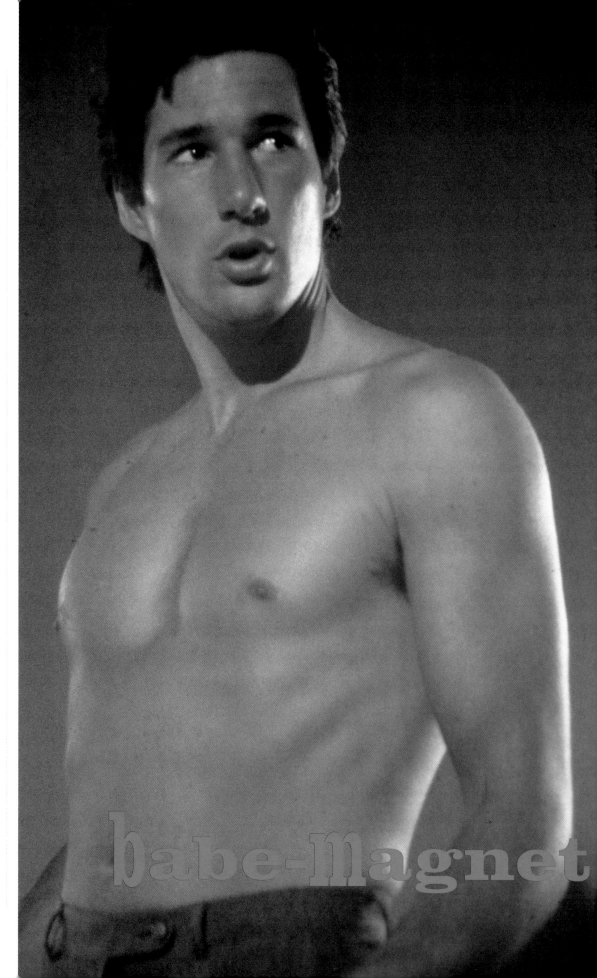

from far left

Antonio Sabato, Jr. (b. 1972)
With his scantily clad image peering over the multitudes from countless billboards, Antonio is fast becoming the '90s version of Michelangelo's statue of David (if he hasn't been so acclaimed already). And he is even more endearing for his open embracing of all his fans (female and male). Is reputed to do 1500 sit-ups a day. Biggest film hit so far: 1998's *The Big Hit*. Best feature: besides the whole "package," a smile that'll send you swooning. Biggest surprise: his gorgeous father, Antonio, Sr., who you can catch a glimpse of in *Grand Prix* (1968). (*Everett Collection*)

Sylvester Stallone (b. 1946)
The first of the Hollywood "muscle-machines," a group that would later include nearly every male star (at one time or another) who could get their hands on a set of weights. From 1970 to 1976, Stallone's career floundered until he had the idea to write the screenplay about a boxer named Rocky Balboa. The rest is history; *Rocky* went on to win the Best Picture Oscar and Stallone became a major force in movie-making. Nice change: going from super "ripped" in *Demolition Man* (1993), et al., to pleasantly plump in *Copland* (1997). (*Everett Collection*)

Jean-Claude Van Damme (b. 1961)
Ably titled the "Muscles from Brussels," this former karate champ can be seen flexing his pecs in a number of popular martial arts films. A sort of Anglo version of Bruce Lee, Jean-Claude worked as a bouncer, carpet-layer, and limo driver, before hitting it big. Famous "pose": his being able to do full leg splits across two countertops. What versatility! (*Everett Collection*)

right

Richard Gere (b. 1949)
Spiritually inclined male "babe" who came to world prominence with his roles in *Days of Heaven* (1978) and *American Gigolo* (1980). It was his performance as the title character in the latter film that would revolutionize the aura of a male lead forever. Beyond the fact that Gere's role was basically that of a male hustler, in reality it said men could (and did) care as much about the way they looked as women. And in that way, it was as much a change for *all* men, as it was for males on-screen. However, Gere's career hit a snag in the mid '80s, bouncing back with 1990's *Pretty Woman* (interesting career-wise, in that costar Julia Roberts played a prostitute to his businessman). Since then he has not left the front ranks. Best look: hanging upside-down in a pair of inversion boots. Remember those? (*Kobal*)

following page

Ty Hardin
(b. 1930, Orson Whipple Hungerford II)
Few film actors, by virtue of their screen roles, so easily fit into one category as Ty does. That's not to say he hasn't appeared as other types of characters, it's just that he was so physically perfect playing a "stud." Beginning in the early '60s, the arc of his popularity, though, was brief. And parts were scarce by the end of the decade. Moving to Spain he was once arrested for possesion of drugs and forced to leave the country. Back in America he became a tele-evangelist. (*Kobal*)

"Before men felt they had to behave like their role models as well as look like them, now he can separate the physical and say he wants to have a great body like Schwarzenegger, but not be interested in modelling the rest of his life after him."
— Michael Lafavore

"*Most people will see what they want to see. If you compete well and look good, they are going to assume that your life is great, when all the while in reality you may be going through a lot of emotional and mental stress. Personally, I went through some rough times, and may have been compulsive and over-acheiving trying to make up for what I felt my life was missing.*"
— Greg Louganis

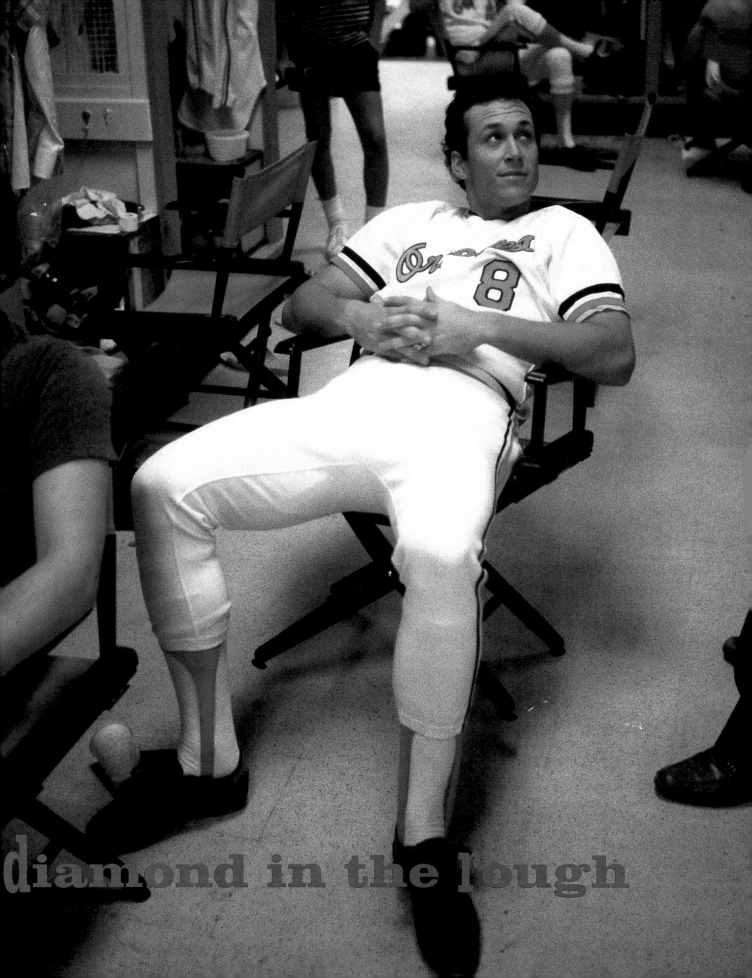

When it comes to pure testosterone-sweating male sex appeal, few can compete with the unabashedly macho allure of a pro-baller, like Deion Sanders or Joe Montana. Aside from the fact that they wear uniforms that seem intentionally designed to exaggerate the male form (wide padded shoulders, narrowed at the waist) to its best advantage, these big lugs never pass up an opportunity to interview half-naked after a game, or pat the firm rear of a teammate during one. How's that for teasing the fans?

I remember reading (or hearing) once, a long time ago, that baseball players were not as physically fit as other athletes, because the lack of constant movement in the game itself. Well, that may or may not be the case, but whoever said it could not have had the good fortune to be stuck in a locker room with such magnificent major-leaguers as Steve Garvey, Tim McCarver, Mickey Mantle, Roger Maris, not to mention Jackie Robinson, Bucky Dent, Tom Seaver, Ken Griffey, Jr., to name a few, or that "daddy" of them all, Jim Palmer.

gridiron galahad

"Men are finally being presented images of what they should look like, the same way women have been for ages. However, men have stonger 'egos' and will always rate their looks (as is) much higher than a woman will about herself."
— Linda Wells

Wayne Gretzky (b. 1961)
Before Gretzky, hockey was a brutish, violent male ritual played out on ice. When Gretzky arrived he gave it a face, and a very nice one at that. (What a sin to lob pucks at that divine kisser!) He also gave the game some much-needed class, softening it a bit, making it almost gentlemanly without losing its aggressive appeal. Of course a pretty face on ice would mean nothing if you couldn't perform—and perform he has. This wavy blond dynamo has led his Edmonton Oilers to four Stanley Cup victories and he himself is the NHL's all-time leader in points, goals, and assists. Sexiest moments: breathless and sweaty after a go-round on the ice. (*Peter Read Miller/Sports Illustrated*)

near left
Michael Jordan (b. 1963)
Is thought to be the greatest sports figure of our time. If you don't agree, you'd have to allow he is the most powerful (or rather influential). With his matinee-idol looks and sophisticated manner he's also poised to conquer Hollywood. No wonder men, women, and children gravitate towards him. But certainly it's more than his muscled frame and shorn, sexy head that attract people. Unquestionably, it's the brains that go with the marvelous package. Well, that and the six NBA title victories he has helped lead his team, the Chicago Bulls, to. Best look: though he's gre-e-e-at in shorts, does a number in a suit. (*John Biever/Sports Illustrated*)

Before these two men came along their respective sports may have been interesting to watch, but not *that* interesting. Afterwards, neither game would ever be the same. Coincidentally, they are both quite the gentlemen, which has frequently helped. pull their teams (and teammates) out of the often brutish and bad-mannered mire we have grown so accustomed to seeing. For that they should receive extra points. A few that should share in their glory: for basketball, Magic Johnson, Scottie Pippen, and, if he's your type, Dennis Rodman; for hockey, Mark Messier and Bobby Hull.

There are few sports with as sexy an aura about them as racing. What with guys like Steve McQueen and Paul Newman taking to the tarmac, how could it not be? However, the fantasy may outpace the reality by a few laps; for all the glamour this is one grueling sport. I mean, imagine yourself going around in circles a couple hundred times and how that would make you feel. Not too pretty. Fortunately, a couple of speedsters have made it out in one piece, like the legendary Mario Andretti and the brash and beautiful upstart, Jeff Gordon.

Boxing is not a sport you would equate with beauty, though there have been a number of comely competitors who have survived the onslaught (with their pretty faces intact). What a miracle! Of the rare who have defied the odds: magnificent Muhammed Ali, exquisite Evander Holyfield, and an outstanding Oscar de la Hoya.

"I like men who combine a little bit of both masculine and feminine traits (and a little bit of eccentricity). I don't like 'macho' men who feel it is their right to intimidate and bully women."
— Naomi Campbell

above
Jeff Gordon (b. 1971)
If they were doing a racing movie and had to cast from people within the sport, Gordon would be the star, hands down. Not since the '60s appeal of sexy Mario Andretti has racing given us a "poster boy" quite on the same caliber as Jeff. Strutting around in black wrap-around sunglasses, dressed in colorful garb that just barely allows for hints of the great bod underneath, he is the "life-imitates-art" real-life hero of all racing movies from *Winning, Days of Thunder,* and *Grand Prix.* At twenty-five, he was the youngest person to ever win the Daytona 500. (*George Tiedemann/Sports Illustrated*)

right
Oscar de la Hoya (b. 1972)
Has the devastating handsomeness and sex appeal that could make any man into a movie star, but he chooses to have his face punched instead. Ouch! Undoubtedly, it better be for a lot of money. (Which it is.) You'd think with a beautiful face like that, other less-so–favored boxers would add jealously to their aggression and be more inclined to do some serious damage. (Hopefully, he'll get out before something irreparable is done.) Olympic gold medal winner in 1992 and 1995 IBF Champion. (*Richard Mackson/Sports Illustrated*)

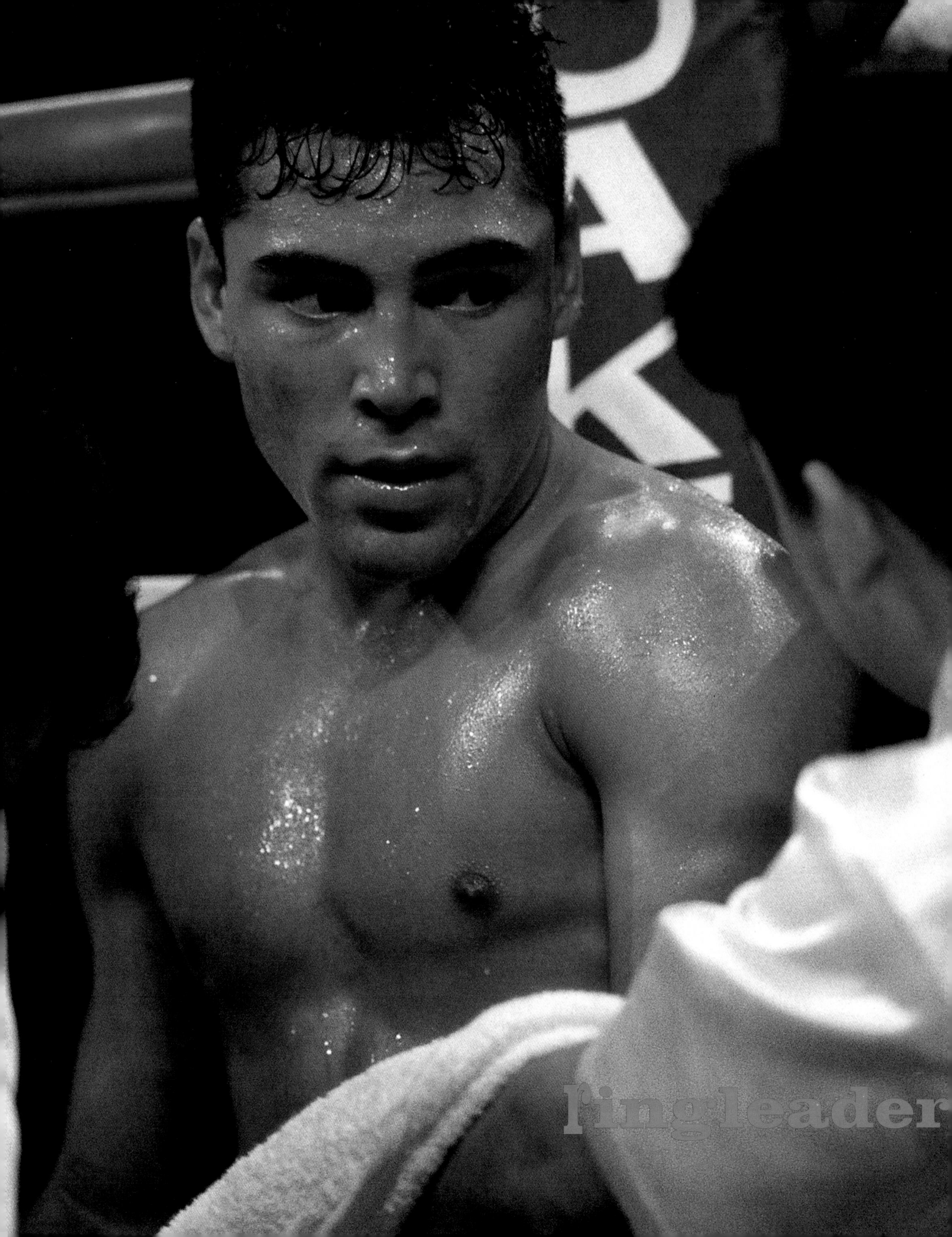
ringleader

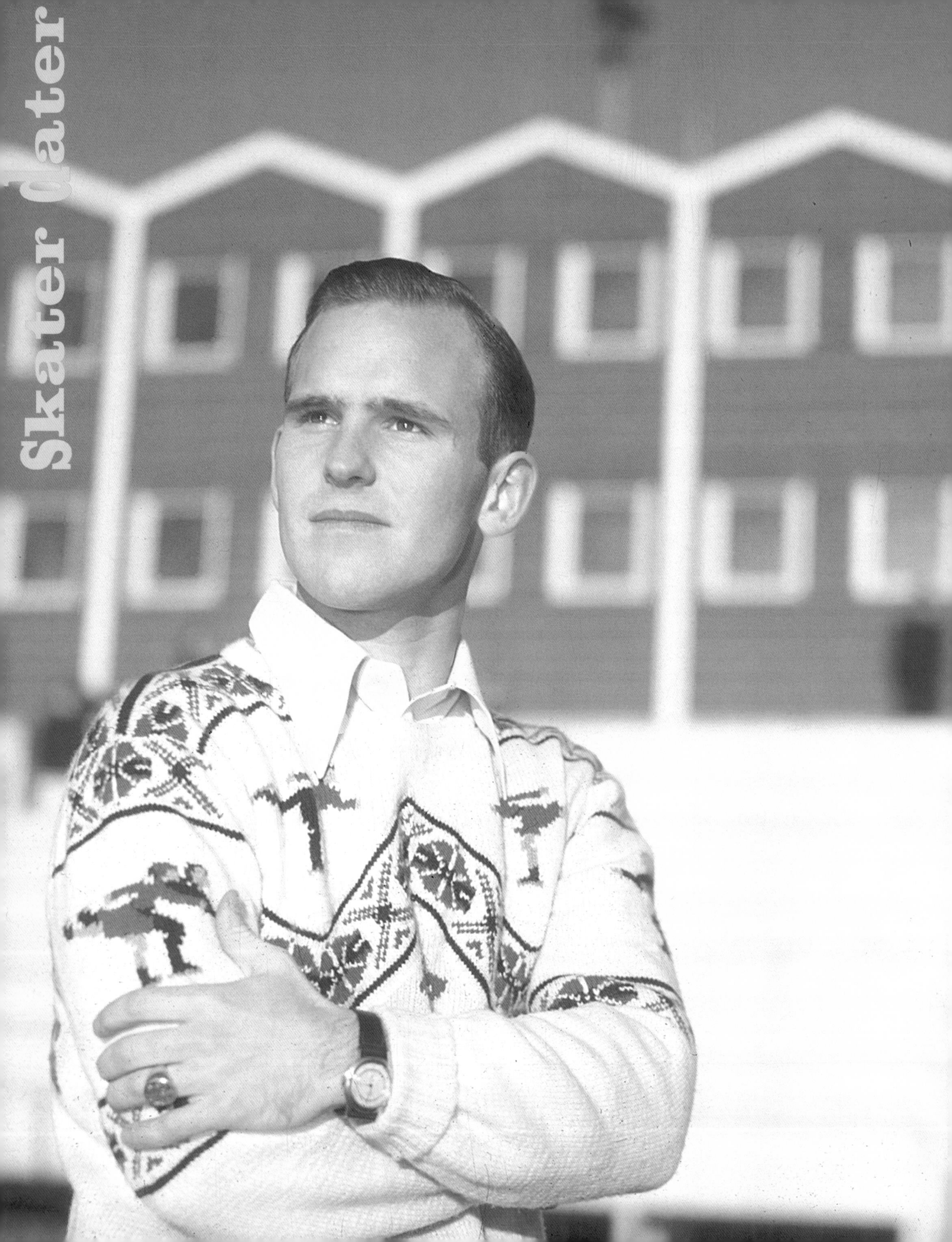
Skater Dater

Both these endeavors are resplendent with examples of the beautiful male, though with very different *types* of men. So, whereas skiing is analogous to water rushing downstream and sometimes over a cliff, and given to brash, bounding, and beefy boys (like Alberto Tomba, Billy Kidd, and Tommy Moe), figure skating is more akin to floating upon a pristine lake with only the occasional whirlwind to contend with, lending itself more to the well-choreographed *and* well-muscled, from Boitano to Browning, Stoyko to Kulik.

far left
Dick Button (b. 1929)
Winning Olympic gold for America in figure skating (twice in succession, 1948-52), Button became the sport's first superathlete. His gentlemanly manner and disarmingly boyish good looks were perfectly suited to the country's idea of a true sports hero and he was honored with the Sullivan Award in 1949, as the year's outstanding amateur athlete. Of late, this still marvelously handsome man has become the favorite of viewers and listeners for his articulate commentary on his chosen sport, even adding an Emmy (for Outstanding Sports Analysis, 1981) to his trophy case. (UPI/Corbis-Bettmann)

above
Jean-Claude Killy (b. 1943)
Upon winning three Olympic golds in 1968, Killy became the skier by which all other able-bodied men would be judged for athleticism and attractiveness forever afterward. He had the cool air of the international sophisticate about him that would prove irresistible to women (and men), in a way that an American skier of equal talent could not compete. It would not be until the ascendency of Italy's swarthily sexy Alberto Tomba in the '80s that Killy's hold on the hearts of ski fans would be seriously challenged, if not necessarily surpassed. (Brian Seed/Sports Illustrated)

Within some circles, the swimmer possesses the most coveted of male physiques, and for good reason. With their long, sinewy limbs and enormous shoulders narrowing down to youthfully small waists they are the perfect blend of the muscular meso and slender endo bodies that so many males wish they had been born with. Oh, what a pleasure it is to watch men like Rowdy Gaines, Matt Biondi, Gary Hall and son, Steve Lundquist, and John Naber part the waters.

To watch divers is to see sculpture in movement. With their beautifully etched, lean, and taut muscular bodies, they are like marble statues come to life. However, their breathtaking journey is fleeting, lasting mere seconds before piercing effortlessly the waters below and ending the dance.

"Because of my accomplishments, I seemed to fit a mold very nicely and uniquely; one that, at the time, was very new and becoming quite popular with the public. Fortunately, the area I came from allowed me to be presented this way without looking contrived or intentional, whereas, if it had been done by a male 'star,' it would be viewed as a publicity stunt. I brought authenticity to wearing a skimpy swimsuit."
— *Mark Spitz*

"The judging in diving is very subjective. In a sport where you hit the water before anyone has had a chance to fully comprehend what you did technically, it's impossible for them not to focus somewhat on what you look like standing on the diving board—it's the most time you'll spend in front of them. Besides, they can see everything—it's very hard to hide in a little Speedo."
— *Greg Louganis*

pool boy

racketeer

Trying to find attractive male tennis players is like shooting fish in a barrel, they are everywhere you turn. From John Newcombe to Jimmy Connors, Ilie Nastase to Andre Agassi, Becker to Bjorg to Sampras, as far back as Bill Tilden (though they are more fun to look at in shorts) and back again, they cover the court like an army of swinging and sweating Adonises. And the faster these guys move across the clay the sexier they become, making you feel like you've just been lobbed in the libido.

The notion is that golf is a gentleman's game (the sport of kings), and that it's played by a lot of stuffy old men in funny pants. Alright, so maybe being a member of the country club is not like working out at the gym in Chelsea, NY, but where is it written that some of them can't be babes? How about a loud Fore! for Greg Norman, Tom Watson, and Jack Nicklaus, not to mention the hottest thing to hit the game in years, Tiger Woods, silly slacks and all.

left
Stephan Edberg (b. 1966)
This Swede was ranked first in the world (in tennis) in 1990 and 1991 and has won Wimbledon, the U.S. Open, and the Australian Open twice each. In a game where being attractive is almost incidental (almost), this Scandinavian "stud" also manages to be a top money-winner, too. Retired in 1996. Best physical asset: what a pair of legs. Puts the "us" in muscle. But that can be said of most male tennis players, right!? *(Jerome Provost; TempSport/Corbis)*

right
Arnold Palmer (b. 1929)
Palmer's ascent in golf was perfectly timed to that of television, giving the sport a look to go with the hero. Boy-next-doorish but somewhat volatile, Arnold always let a bit of emotion show through whenever he played, endearing his fans. For their loyalty they were named "Arnie's Army." Sometimes numbering thirty-thousand, they would follow him everywhere, including overseas tournaments. After winning his last major tournament in the mid '60s (including multiple Masters, U.S. Opens, and British Opens), Palmer still managed to be one of sport's highest-paid athletes even into the '80s by virtue of his many endorsements and commercial appearances. *(Jerry Cooke/Corbis)*

link lochinvar

decathlon don juan

MatMan

Gymnasts, like swimmers and ice skaters, are sports as "living art." They are who Michelangelo would have created if he worked with flesh and blood instead of paint and plaster. And even the great sculptor knew his piece would be ever more memorable if he was rendered with a beautiful face to match the magnificence of his body. A few modern-day Davids: Bart Conner, Kurt Thomas, and Peter Vidmar.

A victorious decathlete is usually also given the title of "World's Greatest Athlete" upon his mastering ten of the most challenging sports known to man. Unarguably, he should add "Most Beautiful" (or handsome, if you prefer) to the inscription too, especially if he's as winsome a warrior as Bruce Jenner, Dan O'Brien, and Rafer Johnson.

Making many other sports seem old-fashioned (competitively and physically) are the games of the "next" generation. From in-line skating, snowboarding to dirt jumping, guys like T. J. Lavin, Jason Borgstede, and David Mirra are a mixed bag of hunky heroes to their rainbow tribe of fans and followers. From this vantage, the future "looks" great.

buff biker

"So much of what made models (male and female) the focus of all this attention in recent years, and beauty in general dominant in our culture, is simply the media (television, films, magazines, etc.) hungry for images to fill their huge, limitless spaces; making it into more than what it is and not because the world necessarily needs to see or understand these things."
— *Cindy Crawford*

"I can appreciate a man caring about the way he looks, but not to the point of him being self-conscious; I prefer a man who feels confident in the way he looks as himself, without the need for artifice or excessive attention."
– Cindy Crawford

Handsome and buffed movie heroes who forsake life and limb to conquer the unconquerable are all fine and dandy, but true-life adventurers show us that the reality of a man in a perilous situation far outshines its effects-enhanced (and stuntman secured) cinematic counterpart. So whether they're on or over the high seas, off scaling a distant mountain peak (nobly like Mr. Hillary), or off into outer space (Houston calling Mr. Glenn), these virile voyagers have ample supplies of the "right stuff."

ardent adventure

Man can shape the shapeless and bind the boundless, take nothing and make it into something. For eons he has walked empty lands and seen cities, crossed miles of open sea and built bridges. Seer, doer, creator *and* destroyer. The most profound of these dreamers changing forever not only their own lives but those of countless others. But whether each of these individuals is a mogul for the millennia or simply a present-day peddler of fortune and flesh, our existence is the wiser for them, for better or worse.

"There isn't an important man from a CEO/board chairman to president of a country, who can't have just about any girl he wants, and he does not have to be good-looking. The same is still not true for a woman. I know a lot who have money and power, but couldn't get arrested in terms of getting a man."
— Helen Gurley Brown

"Playboy had more to do with the freeing of our strict sexual bonds than anything in this century, with its frank display of flesh and edicts on men and how they should live, look and behave. As distasteful as it is for some, schlock can be influential."
— Thomas Hoving

far left
Howard Hughes (1905–76)
America's most (in)famous billionaire recluse, was also at a time, one of the country's handsomest and most eligible bachelors. A businessman, film producer and director, and aviator, handsome Howard inherited his father's machine tool company in 1923, when he was eighteen. Starting in films in 1926, he abruptly left the field for a time to pursue aeronautics, only to return to films in the '40s to launch, among other things, Jane Russell's career in the highly controversial movie, 1943's *The Outlaw*. Hughes was known for squiring some of the most famous and beautiful women of the day, though rumours of his supposed bisexuality have been known to crop up from time to time. Creator and maker of the *Spruce Goose*, a wooden airplane that flew only once but yielded invaluable information to the flying community. (*MPTV Archives*)

left, top
Hugh Hefner (b. 1926)
Editor, creator, and publisher of *Playboy*, unarguably one of the influential magazines of the postwar era. Mixing advice with pictures (both sexual and non in nature), Hugh parlayed his periodical's success into many other areas, including real estate, nightclubs, and various other sundry items, making himself very rich in the process. With his signature pipe and smoking jacket, he was the sexy, urbane role model who spoke to the unconscious yearnings of millions of male readers around the world. (*Everett Collection*)

135

randy royal

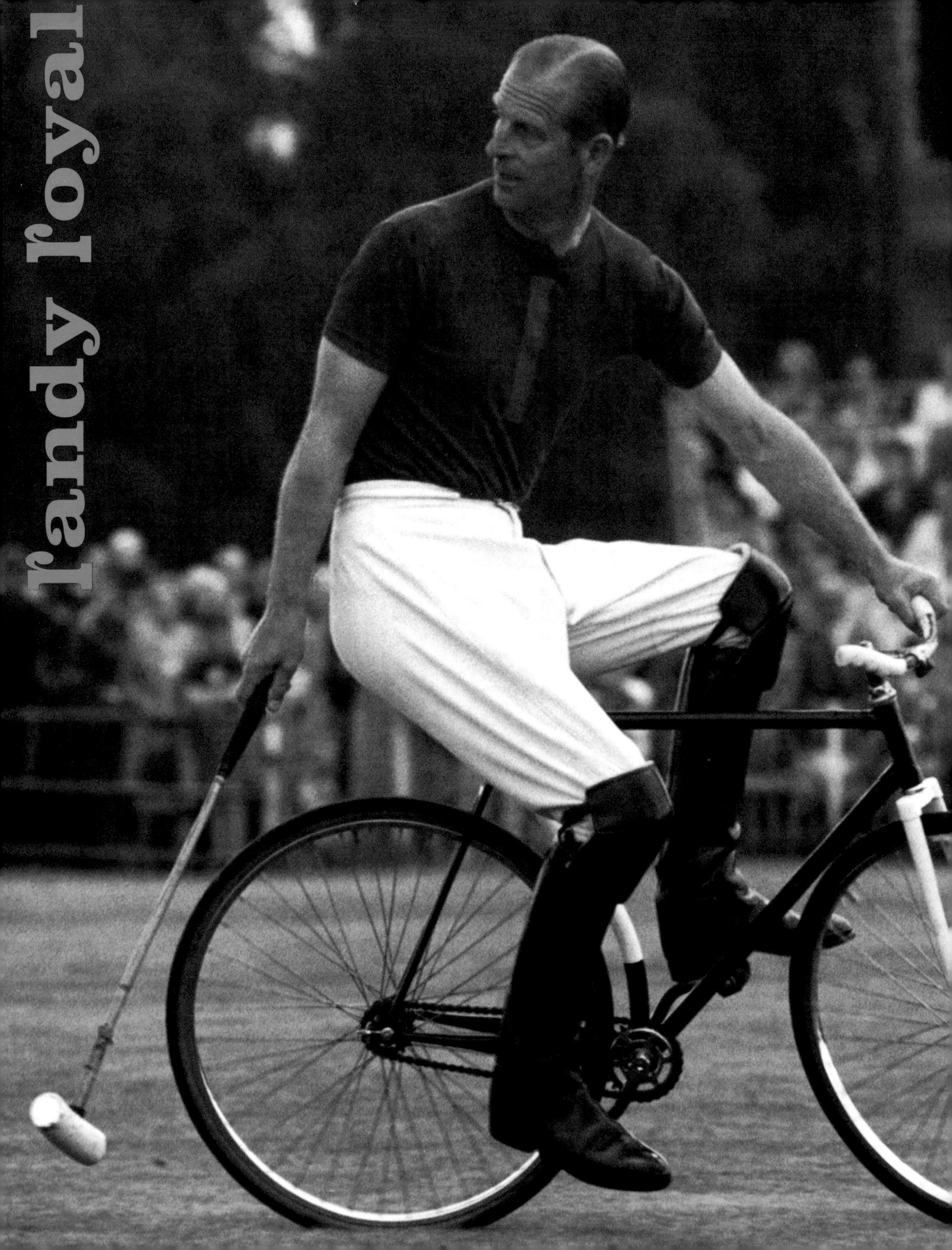

The fantasy is to marry a randy royal and live happily ever after in his castle way up in the clouds. Well, occasionally life behind the guarded walls is not all it's cracked up to be what with all that infighting and *in*breeding. But it is still good to be king (*and* the king's consort), presiding over those fancy functions and finery, not forgetting all those divine common (and not so common) folk bowing, curtsying, and catering to your *every* whim. If only there were more monarchs to go around.

left, top
Prince Phillip, Duke of Edinburgh
(b. 1921)
Born in Corfu, Phillip's father was Prince Andrew of Greece and his mother was Princess Alice of Battenberg. When he was young, Phillip was a stunner with his wavy blond hair, handsome face, and athletic build. He joined the Royal Navy in 1939, married Elizabeth in 1947, becoming a naturalized citizen. A statesman, yachtsman, and airman, his heartthrob good looks filtered down the family tree to his grandson, Prince William, son of Prince Charles and the late Lady Diana Spencer. (*Hulton-Deutsch/Corbis-Bettmann*)

right
King Juan Carlos I of Spain
(b. 1938)
King of Spain from 1975, Carlos was born in Rome and is the grandson of Spain's last ruling monarch, Alphonso the Eighth. In 1962, he married Princess Sophia of Greece; they have three children, including an absolutely gorgeous boy (like father, like son). Named by leader Franco to be his successor, he presided over Spain's democratization. (*Graphic House/Corbis-Bettmann*)

"Traditionally, we chose mates to make up for what we didn't have. Men had money and houses, which women didn't, but we had beauty, which men got by wearing us."
—Nancy Friday, from her book, The Power of Beauty

"Whatever it is that's special about you to another person automatically makes you beautiful to them."
—Claudia Schiffer

presidential prowess

far left

Ronald Reagan (b. 1911)
Our nation's fortieth president. Went to Hollywood in 1937 and made over fifty films, including the fantastic *King's Row* (1941) and the silly *Bedtime for Bonzo* (1951), before turning completely to politics, beginning as president with the Screen Actors Guild in 1947. A real "looker" in his early days, this eight-year California governor named his autobiography, *Where's the Rest of Me,* his most famous line of screen dialogue (from *King's Row*). Most endearing physical characteristic: a hairstyle that hasn't moved an inch since his start in film. (*Kobal*)

left

John F. Kennedy (1917–63)
America's thirty-seventh president. Undeniably the nation's most charismatic and attractive first leader was also responsible for bringing the libido into the White House, for which you can thank him or hate him. Also the first Catholic and youngest president (the latter being a great influence on his physical attraction). Was an advocate of human rights and the space race. His 1956 book *Profiles in Courage* won the Pulitzer Prize. A sign of great genes: a whole family tree full of handsome and beautiful men. (*Black Star*)

right, bottom

John F. Kennedy, Jr. (b. 1960)
Possibly the most famous "son" in the country. Certainly one of the most visibly attractive, much to his chagrin. It seems that no matter how hard "John-John" tries to be thought of for something other than his fortuitous parentage, his image appears on the cover of another magazine, heralding his traffic-stopping good looks. (But with a face like that, who can blame them.) The publisher of the post-modern periodical *George,* John broke many-a-heart when he wed Carolyn Bessette in 1996. Though nothing lasts forever, right? (*Black Star*)

If both your parents are attractive, chances are we'll *all* end up lucky and the heavens will send down one of their own to walk among us. Now he'll have a hard time living up to the expectations we (and his parents) have of him, and just because he is of such celestial birth, doesn't necessarily mean he'll be especially nice, overly smart, or just more than a little fun to talk to. But with a face and body like that who's worried about intelligent conversation?

Holding office as the most powerful man in the world is, as we well know, quite an overwhelming aphrodisiac. So much so that you don't have to be especially handsome, well-built, or young to get what other men couldn't even pay for. And, sometimes, the guy in the Oval Office *is* a real catch, meaning no disrespect for the position or the person, who just happens to be the country's top executive. How's that for being in the right place at the right time?

"Beauty is so much more relative today; the choices are endless. The man can be a dog, but if he's saying, thinking or wearing the right thing, he can be so-o-o attractive."
— Isaac Mizrahi

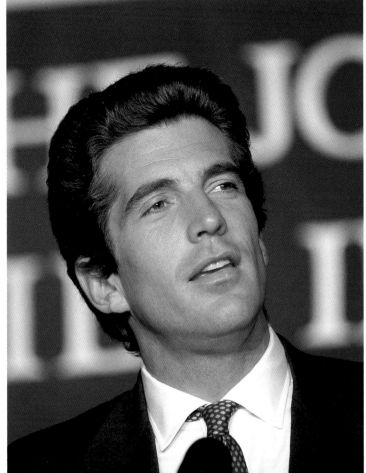

Although the intention is that their *words* are supposed to make us think of beautiful thoughts, rare is the individual who can pass up a jacket photo if it has one of these scholars pictured therein. And what literary journey isn't made more enjoyable, with the knowledge that the captain of the boat is as virile as his vernacular. A few "lions" of lore: Ernest Hemingway (pre- or post-"surly" seafarer), the two beefy "beats" of the '5os, Jack Kerouac and Neal Cassady, and the "gentle" giant, Michael Crichton.

near right

Sebastian Junger (b. 1963)
Despite literary success with his best-selling book, *The Perfect Storm*, Sebastian is having a hard time getting people to focus on his work and not his body (but with that face it may be a losing battle). As much an outdoorsman as he is an author, he lives exactly the type of lifestyle you would expect for such a rugged guy. His next works are, not surprisingly, expected to take place in war-torn areas of Central America and Sri Lanka. Overwhelming realization: just too sexy for his own good. (*Photo by Christopher Kolk/Outline*)

right

Tom Tryon (1926–91)
Yale-educated, this hunk gave up success as an actor (including an Oscar nomination for 1963's *The Cardinal*) to become a writer. With best-sellers like *The Other* and *Crowned Heads*, it seems as though he knew what he was doing. This big slice of beefcake is proof that fame in Hollywood isn't always a trap and that there are alternatives. (*MacFadden/Corbis-Bettmann*)

"Beauty can take you only so far, but put together with brightness, intelligence, and a sense of humor there are no limits."
—*Naomi Campbell*

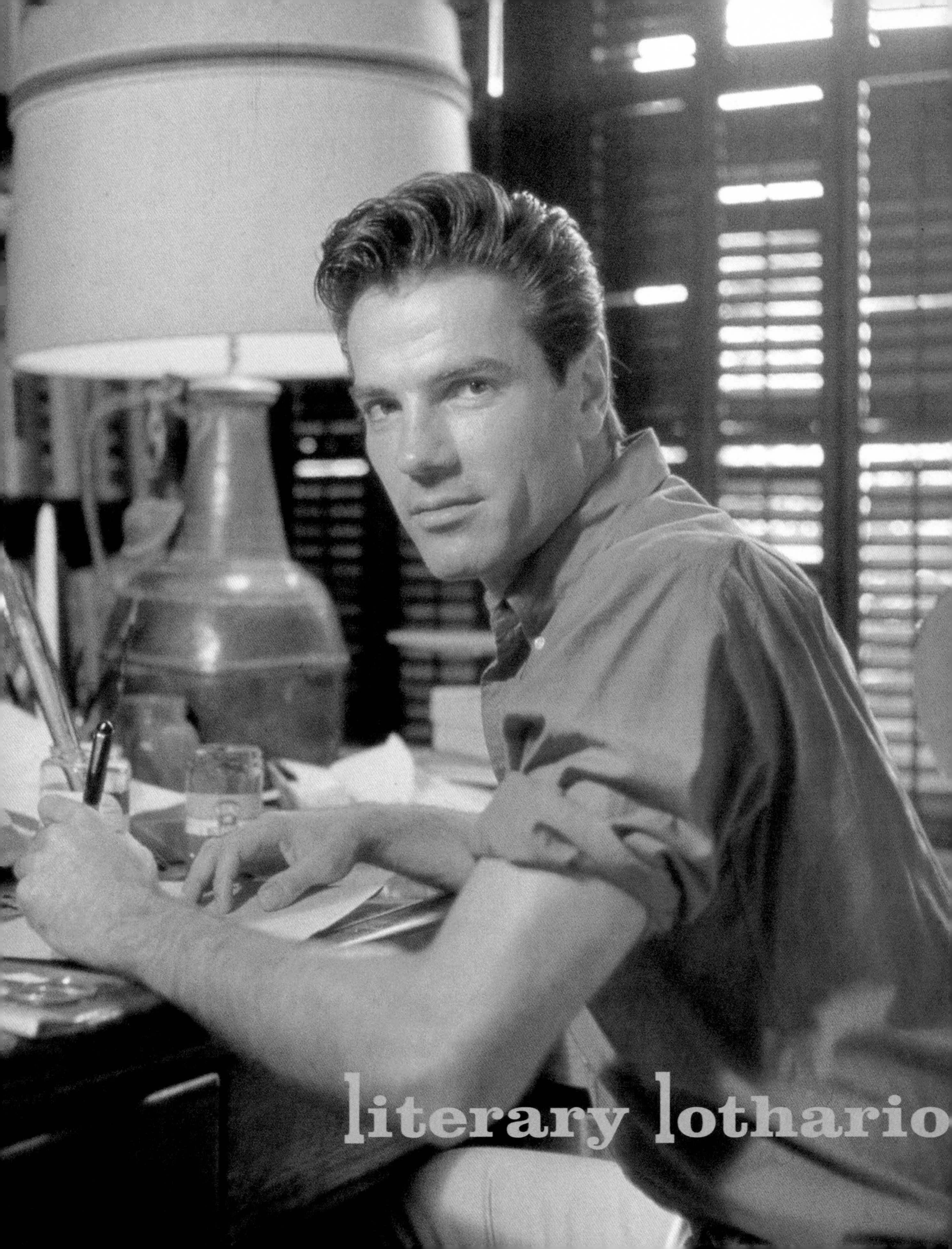

literary lothario

lusty lensman

Just because a person chooses to place himself behind the camera instead of in front of it does not mean they have anything to hide. And in reality, you're likely to find quite a handful of stunners peering through the lens of a camera, channeling whatever beautiful thoughts that surround them into pictures (both still and moving) for the rest of us to enjoy. For this we should be forever thankful. Besides, most directors and photographers are no more extroverted than either you or I (and we can't all hog the spotlight). However, though modesty, too, is an admirable trait, there are a few head-turners in this camera-ready category—including Nick Cassavetes, David Fincher, Herb Ritts, Phil Joanou, and Sante D'Orazio, among others—that no one would *ever* have a problem giving a second glance.

left
John Sayles (b. 1950)
This Williams College grad went on to win two O. Henry Awards for short stories before moving on to screenwriting, including penning, of all things, *Piranha* (1978) and *The Howling* (1980). However, it was upon his directorial debut in 1979, with *The Return of The Secaucus Seven*, that John's true destiny was revealed. Garnering much praise for this first effort, sexy Sayles has continued to make his mark (as director, often screenwriter, and occasional actor) with small, intimate, and thoughtful films. (*Everett Collection*)

right
Franco Zefferelli (b. 1923)
Stage, opera, and film director whose keen eye managed to take the unworkable and make it palatable to the masses. Famous for his discovery of young talent, including lavishing unheard-of camera time to a breathtakingly nude and beautiful Leonard Whiting in 1968's smash filming of *Romeo and Juliet*, Franco is as handsome as his young charges. Of his numerous films, including the Burton and Taylor version of *Taming of the Shrew* (1967), is the Brooke Shield's picture, *Endless Love* (1981), with Martin Hewitt for you boy-watchers, and Mel Gibson's star turn in *Hamlet* (1990). (*Everett Collection*)

"In order to get a good picture often it's not enough if the guy just has a pretty face or a great body; he's got to be able to bring something else from his personality into the image to make it memorable."
—*Herb Ritts*

It was not so long ago, back during the dawn of television some forty-odd years ago, that people on the small screen had to really look the part they were playing. So, if you were the "head of the house" you looked like Robert Young or Danny Thomas; if you were the "college boy" you looked like Richard Crenna or Dwayne Hickman. And even outside of acting, your appearance needed to convey the *right* message. Then if you were a newscaster you definitely had to look like Edward R. Murrow or Walter Cronkite. (Not to say there's anything wrong with that, because these men were *quite* solid, to say the least.) But it wouldn't

be too long before network executives realized the quickest way into a viewer's head (and eventually into their pockets) was through the eyes. And the more people will come, the comelier the man. But my, how things have changed from where we began. It's a regular beefcake beauty contest out there (although you'll get no complaints here!) However, the big question always is, is there anything substantial behind the fab facades? My feeling is—who would you rather get your bad news, lousy weather forecast, or the latest video countdown from?

A short list of TV
"traffic stoppers:"

Charlie Rose
Stone Phillips
Peter Jennings
Tom Brokaw
Brian Williams
Kevin Newman
Dan Rather
Jack Ford

*"People's issues about
beauty are incredibly
personal, even though
the formulas seem so
public."*
– Ingrid Sischy

designing Men

left, top
Jean Louis (b. 1907–95)
This hunk was one of Tinseltown's finest cou-
turiers and put some of the most sumptuous
gowns ever created on the likes of Marilyn
Monroe. Something to ponder: isn't Jean
looking a lot like a '50s version of Isaac
Mizrahi in this picture? (*Kobal*)

left, bottom
Adrian (1903–59)
This "boy-next-door" was responsible for the
look of all the top female stars of the
"Golden Age" of Hollywood, including
Crawford, Shearer, Garbo, et. al. Left the film
business after being forced to design "ordinary" clothes, and started his own label. Was
once married to star Janet Gaynor. His last
costume design job was for the stage version
of *Camelot*. This magnificent tailor sadly com-
mitted suicide. Trademark look: the shoulders
in his women's jackets, especially for Joan.
(*Everett Collection*)

right
Tom Ford
Designer as sex symbol. As magnificent as his
clothes are for Gucci (which he brought back
into the forefront of fashion), it is hard to
ignore the sheer physical appeal of the man
himself. No doubt he is as good an advertisement for his wares as any male model could
be. And besides, he really knows what to
leave "out" of a piece of clothing. (*Photo courtesy of Gucci*)

Designers used to be happy
making *other* people look
beautiful. Well, that's our
loss, because we've missed
seeing some tempting tai-
lors. Thank goodness the
emergence of sportswear
changed all that. Before you
may have had designer
houses and might have
known a few names, but
never a face to go with the
label. Then with the acceptance of ready-to-wear people were anxious to thank
the makers, personally. So
out from behind the curtain
walked such sublime seam-
sters as Halston, Calvin
Klein, Giorgio Armani,
Thierry Mugler, Perry Ellis,
Bob Mackie, and Gianni
Versace.

*"Men have more per-
sonal style than women,
not meaning they have
better taste; they know
what looks best on
them, because they have
always worked with a
more limited amount of
options. However, in
terms of 'changing'
their looks, dress, and
style, men have to walk
before they run, where-
as women can run
before they walk."*
— *Jim Moore*

There are really only three distinct periods of male modelling; the entire period before the '70s, the '70s into the early '80s, and now (or rather the last ten years). Interestingly, but not too surprisingly, these periods line up with social changes in our society (much as changes in the male physique does). Before the '70s men modelled, but it wasn't a profession to be particularly proud of, because men (for all of those decades) were not supposed to be *too* interested in how they looked (even though they were), therefore a man who's lifework it was to be photographed in clothes (or out of them) was somewhat disenfranchised. Nor were male models *especially* handsome or beautiful, because no real man could accept being attracted to any advertisement in general, let alone one with a gorgeous guy staring out at him. So the emphasis was on the manlier type, like the Marlboro Man or Hathaway shirt fellow. Or better yet, men in advertising were frequently illustrated. Now, how's that for a twist? With the guy not being real at all, that left the male consumer free to secretly fantasize about the product or image *any* way he chose to, without the guilt. Well, this silliness lasted for what must have seemed an interminable amount of time until those marvelous sexual revolutions came along (during the late '60s and early '70s) and things were definitely going to change, forever. Now we had women and gay men banding together (whether they knew it or not), saying they must be recognized, respected, and reckoned with. Some of what we got for our efforts (good or bad) was a change in the male persona. Slow at first (remember, we were coming from a place of a lot of denial), it built to a point, where, by the end of the decade, many of our coffers were full of gorgeous men, most nearly naked and many willing to go *either* way. Ah, the glorious days of disco! This phenomena was ably reflected in the magazines we bought and the advertisements we saw in them. Madison Avenue knew a good thing, and so began the first epoch of male modelling, as we know it today. New York City streets (not to mention Los Angeles and Paris and Milan) were strewn with the bodies of beauteous men ready to have their picture taken or their clothes taken off (as is evident in the multitudes of male flesh showing up in places as new and varied as *Playgirl*, *Cosmopolitan*, *After Dark*, *Viva* [remember that one] and *Gentlemen's Quarterly*). Of course, there were still the stalwarts like *Esquire*, but for connoisseurs of this type of thing, it was a field day. For gay men, it was the first time we began to see ourselves (would that we were all that gorgeous) and could even name our favorite male models, behaving not unlike our sisters and their teen "idols." From Jeff Aquilon to Matt Collins, Rick Edwards to Bill Curry, Reginald White to Michael Ives, Michael Harder, and so on, each one of them was someone's favorite. This was also the time men's sportswear came up in the ranks and the beginning of all those magnificent menswear ads, like Gianni Versace's (which have always been cause for celebration), as well as the most revelatory, revealing, and resplendent of them all, those for Calvin Klein, photographed by Bruce Weber. In fact, it was the images created

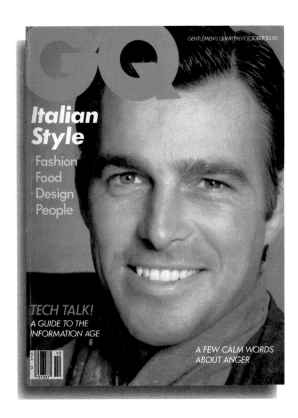

"*Getting into modelling was nothing I planned, I just fell into it. But it was hard in the beginning; people always asked me if I was the messenger — that sort of thing. Now I'm seen as a type of role model, although I don't necessarily feel like one. It's also changed the way I do my job. I used to just go and pose for a picture; now those photos have to stand for something.*"
— *Tyson Beckford*

"*There is much more of a visual range in what women find physically attractive in a man, as opposed to what men find good-looking in a woman. Moreover, for women it's not about looking at a picture of a beautiful man, it's too one-dimensional and doesn't provide enough information. For men it's much simpler, they see it in a magazine and want it.*"
— *Linda Wells*

by Weber and his magnificent subjects, that took the obvious (albeit almost invisible up to that point) and made it special; men are beautiful, and photograph thusly. Fortunately, with such able practicioners, enthusiasts were able to weather the onslaught of the '80s conservatism that rushed in as soon as the "decadent decade" ended. Trying mightily to vanquish all evidence that pretty men existed at all, they put on their own show of power "playing" with their very own manly action heros figures. Not that there was physically anything wrong, necessarily, about all that testosterone; it just needed some deflating now and then. Thank goodness those handsome male models never left us, though the spotlight was often blocked by their bullish brethren. Male mannequins did suffer one singularly significant, though not insurmountable, setback with a slight format change at *Gentleman's Quarterly*. From late 1983, the veritable men's magazine stopped using male models on their covers, preferring to shoot celebrity/personality types (like sports players and actors), making the few years prior, for many, something of a "golden age" itself for masculine modelling. (I hope I still have mine somewhere.) This too, unofficially, ended the second period of male modelling. Enter the third period, with the slack created by *GQ* being picked up eventually by other men's periodicals (notably *Men's Health* and *Details*) and together with astounding photographs from lensmen like Herb Ritts and Steven Meisel, and continually Bruce Weber, a new "renaissance" of male beauties (and images) began to resurface by the end of the decade. (However, it must be noted that *GQ* did not stop using male models. In fact, it used fabulous new upstarts like John Pearson splendidly in countless editorial shoots.) Into the '90s flowed these images, buoyed by the strength of ever-expanding men's clothing and toiletries markets, as well as the acceptance of the gay community's financial clout and women's insurgence into previously male-dominated fields. All this created an arena that demanded their existence. That, and not forgetting these simple truths if you are selling a product (which is, after all, what a model does): Gay men like to look at good-looking men, as do straight women, and will spend in areas that attract them. Straight women, for the most part, still buy their men their clothing. And, straight men will eventually *openly* embrace their own physicality (and all that entails), understanding that doing so doesn't make them any less of a man.

STARCHED OR SOFT, the

Arrow

*mark is a dependable indicator
of a satisfactory* COLLAR

CLUETT, PEABODY & CO. Inc. Makers, Troy, N.Y.

"When you're in the business you have to work with the type of man who is in demand. However, that doesn't mean he is necessarily going to be attractive to you or me."
— Eileen Ford

"I think all those men's underwear ads are the '90s version of the 'Charlie' spots from the '70s (the one's where the woman pinches the man on his bottom) and there to amuse and empower women, not necessarily to titillate, because I still don't think we look at a picture of a semi- (or fully) nude man in the same way that men look at a photo of a naked woman."
— Cindy Crawford

GUCCI
underwear

Christopher Reeve (b. 1952)

left

One of the handsomest men to ever grace the silver screen. In an age (the late '70s) when matinee idols were fast becoming scarce, Reeve's appearance was a revelation. Tall, blue-eyed, and of dark wavy hair, this muscular beauty was the perfect choice to play one of pop culture's most beloved figures, Superman. That Reeve loved to act, both on-screen and onstage, also made him more than just another pretty face. But the irony is not lost that the screen's favorite superhero should be so tragically rendered earthbound by a riding accident. Now however, his courageous spirit makes him every bit the real-life hero we expected him to be. Has recently turned ably to directing. Most riveting moment on film: his "kissing scene" in *Deathtrap* (1982), which also showed he was not afraid to take on a controversial role, too. (*Everett Collection*)

right, top

Sean Connery (b. 1930)

By the time Connery uttered his famous lines, ". . . Bond, James Bond," in the first of a series of films he would do as the best incarnation of Ian Fleming's superspy, men (young and old) knew exactly who they wanted to be and women knew exactly what they wanted their men to look like. Despite this overwhelming identification he would have with this one character, this sexy Scot has never had too much trouble finding roles outside the espionage arena, including a much-deserved Oscar-winning turn in 1987's *The Untouchables*. Interestingly, though he has for years been considered one of the world's sexiest men, he's always hated the role that brought him to stardom. Best physical feature: the most beautifully (and symmetrically) hairy chest to ever be photographed on film. Period. (*Kobal*)

right, bottom

Randolph Scott (1898–1987)

How's this for the American hero-type: Scott at fourteen, lied about his age to enter into service in WWI. After combat duty, he earned a degree in engineering, but surprisingly turned to acting upon graduation. Fortuitously, his strapping good looks and rugged build would make him an ideal screen presence. His film career was launched after a chance meeting with Howard Hughes in 1927, and though he was first a romantic lead, he became best-known as a star of westerns. Scott was also one of Hollywood's savviest business men, and upon his retirement in the '60s was one of the community's richest men, with a fortune topping out at around one-hundred million. Pretty as a postcard: made a stunning visual counterpart to his onetime roommate, equally handsome Cary Grant. (*Author's collection*)

If role models like movie and sports stars weren't enough to make a guy feel inadequate, as well as male models too gorgeous to be believed, we'd have to add figures of fiction to the list of men's anxiety-makers. Were it not that they are so beautifully drawn (like Green Lantern comics in the '70s) or memorably written (like Ian Fleming's Agent 007), maybe then they wouldn't be half as attractive to us, keeping in mind, these fabulous-looking fellows were created almost exclusively for the *literal* consumption of other men. So, not unlike illustrations for men's goods, or really good-looking guys in television surrounded by buxom babes (like the dudes in "Baywatch"), this vicarious living through our superheroes allows for the usage without any of the answerability.

"All throughout this century, this idea of what masculine beauty is has been constantly influenced by heterosexual men's fears. Women gaining equality and the emergence of gay males are regarded as general threats to their masculinity; so they go to an extreme again and bump the physical ideal up another level."
—*Michelangelo Signorile*

starting from left to right

Gordon Scott (b. 1927)
The handsomest of the dark-haired jungle "kings," Scott was once, not surprisingly, a fireman and lifeguard. (*Author's collection*)

Johnny Weismuller (1904–84)
The most famous (and successful) of all the screen Tarzans, this Olympic gold-medal-winner (five in total) swung through a dozen of the adventure pictures. Great fleeting moments: glimpses of his gluteus maximus muscles that revealed a lot more than the censors were ever comfortable with. (*Kobal*)

Miles O'Keefe (b. 1954)
Though our hothouse hunk has been seen many, many times, including recently with gorgeous Casper Van Dien, it is the sight of magnificently muscled O'Keefe in the 1981 installment *Tarzan the Ape Man* that almost sends all the rest of these hunks back to the gym. Va-va-va-voom. Puts the "pec" in spectacular. (*Everett Collection*)

Lex Barker (1913–73)
The man who took over from Weismuller was easily the most handsome of them all, though his sensational looks may have been better suited to more traditional roles. But with a body and face like that, no one is complaining. Once married to Arlene Dahl and Lana Turner. Prettiest feature: his wonderfully wavy, blond hair. (*Kobal*)

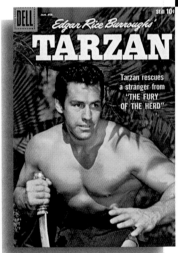

"A man is truly beautiful when he is comfortable within himself, when he knows the power of his spirit and the natural sensuality of his body."
— *Donna Karan*

What book on gorgeous guys would be complete without a homage to the most wantonly sexual male of them all, Tarzan? When Edgar Rice Burroughs first took pen to paper and created our hunky hero in 1914, little did he know that over eighty years later the jungle giant would still be going strong. From Mike Henry to Ron Ely, Jock Mahoney to Christopher Lambert, Elmo Lincoln to Casper Van Dien, all of us have our favorite. It will be interesting to see, with his lush habitat fast disappearing, where he'll be swinging those oiled loins in the next century.

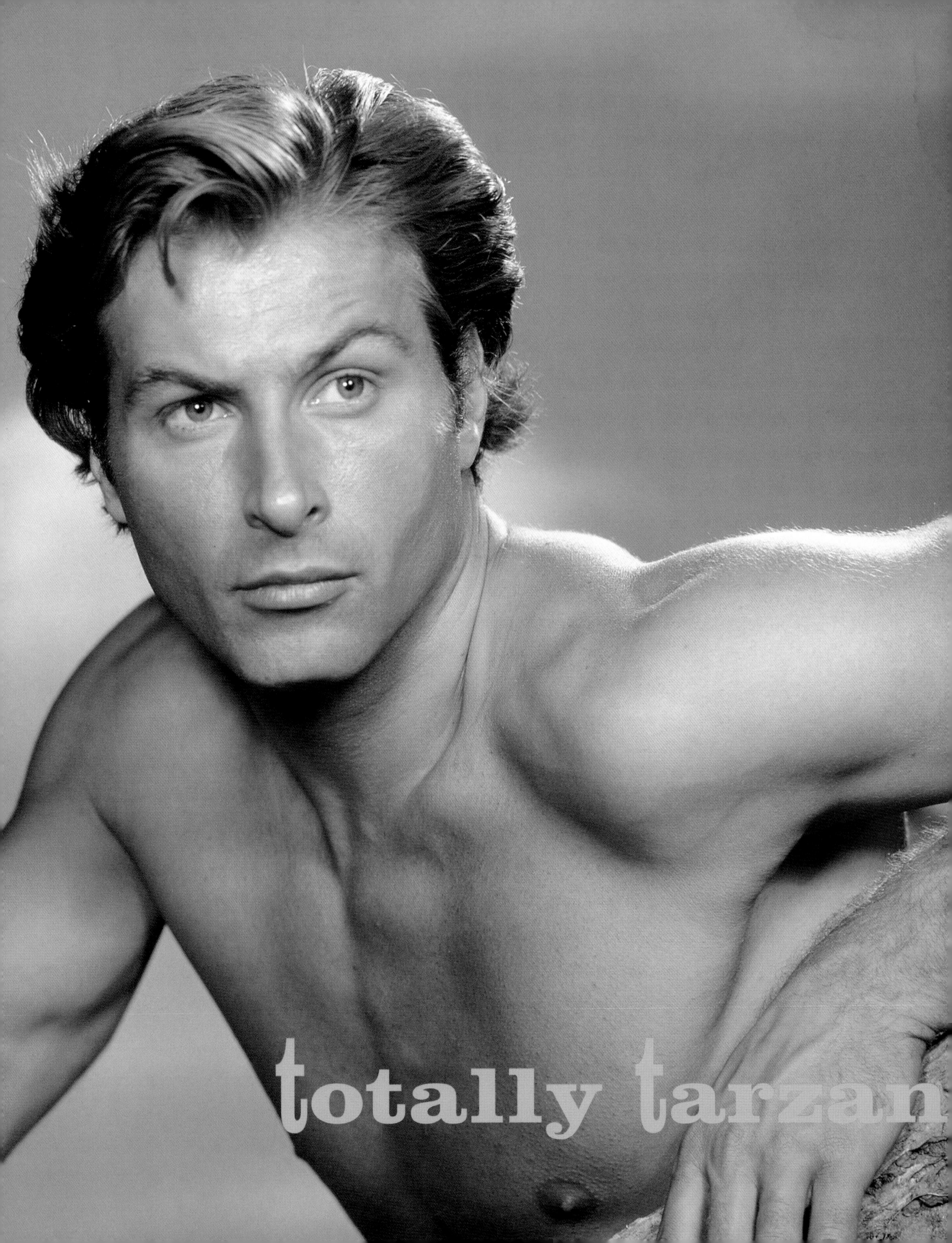
totally tarzan

right
Bruce Lee (1940–73)
It's a real shame that there is a lack of ethnic male sex symbols in this book, however, for the most part that was the reality of the situation. Furthermore, it was impossible to find a well-known Asian male sex symbol, with the exception of Lee. Thankfully, he did exist, and without a doubt, he was an absolutely splendid-looking man. Starting out with marginal success in America, most memorably as Kato in television's *Green Hornet*, a beautifully buff Bruce had to move to Hong Kong (to star in a series of martial arts films) to become a star. What he became was a legend. The most famous of his "chop-socky" movies being 1973's *Enter the Dragon*, which was released the year of his mysterious death. His legacy lived on for a time in the resplendent embodiment of his equally gorgeous son, Brandon (1965-93). But that too would be short-lived, as young Brandon was accidentally killed (by a prop gun) while filming the 1994 movie *The Crow*. (MPTV Archives)

"I know they're saying that modelling has become more racially diverse, but as far as the men are concerned I couldn't name more than one black model (Tyson) and I don't even know of any really big Asian or Hispanic men at all. Besides, things have just started to open up on the women's side and within my industry they don't like to take risks. Their feeling is 'if they don't see it, it doesn't exist.' I think we still have a long way to go before we can truthfully say things have changed."
—*Naomi Campbell*

left
James Franciscus (1933–91) Possibly James was too handsome for great film and television success, although that didn't stop him from trying. Not too shabbily, this Yale-educated dreamboat managed to headline five small-screen series, though none for longer than two seasons, and appear in dozens of pictures. So effortlessly filled out the loincloth vacated by Charlton Heston in the second film of that series, *Beneath the Planet of the Apes* (1970). *(MacFadden/Corbis-Bettmann)*

following page
Rory Calhoun (b. 1922) Hollywood scuttlebutt says that Calhoun's career was railroaded by a studio anxious to cover for another star. The story goes that he was offered up as the sacrificial lamb to squelch revelatory rumours that fellow actor Rock Hudson was homosexual (which of course he was). Whether or not the scandal (involving Rory's brush with the law) actually hurt his success may be impossible to measure, although it is amazing that a man so drop-dead handsome did not become an even bigger star than he was. A wonderful male addition in *With A Song In My Heart* (1952) and *How to Marry a Millionaire* (1953). And, if you like that '50s Brylcreem look: he had a beautiful full head of wavy jet-black hair. *(MacFadden/Corbis-Bettmann)*

The author would first like to thank his editor, Abby Wilentz, for being so understanding and patient, and for enduring his endless diatribes on the questionable "merits" of a picture book of pretty men. I am grateful for her open-mindedness and friendship. To Charles Miers, our publisher, for seeing those "merits," and still letting it go on to be printed. And to the entire staff at **Universe** for helping me to realize a professional goal and take a step out from "behind the curtain." To my **Alias** partner Jed Root for helping to open those doors and, in this particular case, allowing me to do what I needed in order to be satisfied with the work. Thank you. I also want to thank the entire staff of his own company, **Jed Root, Inc.**, for assisting whenever the instance came up.

To Joe and Dan, Tony, Miisa and Lee, Teresa and Scott, Lou, Mark, Darlene and John, to Jeff and Eddie, Peter and John, Kevyn and Eric, Greg, Jim and Gary, Wayne, Mitch and Harris, thank you for your unending friendship and support of my work. To my family, Mom, Dad, Jan and Tom, and Len (especially Mom and Janet for influencing the choices made in this book, whether they knew it or not). I could not have done this without any one of you behind me. Finally, I want to thank Red (and his gang of merrymakers) for their humor and companionship. And most especially, I must thank my own personal "heartthrob," Robert, for putting up with all my neuroses and idiosyncracies, bad moods, and long hours. You'll never know how happy I am to have you in my life.

This book was also made possible by the help, support and inspiration of the following individuals and organizations: Vince Aletti, Constantine Baris, Shelly Bacote, Lina Bey, Christina Bonder, Ashley Brokaw, Yen Bui and the entire staff at **MPTV Archives**, Dick Button, Karen Carpenter, Jennifer Casden, Patty Cohen, Bob Cosenza and the entire staff at **Kobal**, Warren Cowan, Norman Curry and the entire staff at **Corbis-Bettmann**, Joan Deignan, Meryl Delierre and Eve Povzea and the entire staff at **Everett**, Sante D'Orazio, Kristin Dugovic, Sara Foley, Alan Foshko, Jill Fritzo, Mike Gallagher, Lisa Getz, Laura Giammarco, Alan Glasser, Robert Garlock, Kelly Graham, Desiree Gruber, A. J. Hammer, Joyce Hindlin, Lisa Hintelmann, Beth Ann Holden, Lisa Jacobson, Jim Johnson, Van Johnson, Jennifer Josephy, Mark Kerrigan and **Celebrity Services**, Vivien Labaton, Judy Lawne, Bob Levine, Rachel Lizerbran, John Lum and the staff at **Comzone**, Bob Mackie, Kevin Mancuso, April Martin, Lynn Matsumoto, Susan McDermott, Mark McKenna, Lorraine Mead, Steven Meisel, Howard Mendelbaum, the staff at **Michael Ochs Archives**, Shanin Molinaro, Russell Nardoza, Missie Neville, Amy Richards, Andrew Rose, Conrad Rippy, Sandra Rubalcava, Lissette Santiago, Rocky Schenk, Anne Schneider, Kitt Shapiro, Sophia Seidner, Elina Smith, Patty Smith, Barbara Stone, Pat Storey, Freyda Tavin, Michael Thompson, Jennifer Trauth, Yuen Kee Tse, Margaret Van Buskirk, Lisa Vasquez, Holly Wilkinson, Roy Windham of **Baby Jane of Hollywood**, Sandy Wissell, Kaelin Woods, thank you all.

The following publications were used as reference materials for *Heartthrob*:

The 1998 ESPN Information Please Sports Almanac
Halliwell's Filmgoer's Companion (Twelfth Edition)
Chambers Biographical Dictionary (Sixth Edition)
Total Television: The Comprehensive Guide to Programming from Past to Present by Alex McNeil
The Virgin Encyclopedia of Popular Music by Colin Larkin
The Power of Beauty by Nancy Friday
The Film Lover's Companion edited by David Quinlan
The Film Encyclopedia by Ephraim Katz
The Big Book of Show Business Awards by David Sheward
A Who's Who of Sports Champions by Ralph Hickok
The Billboard Book of Top-40 Hits (Sixth Edition) by Joel Whitburn
Our Times, The Illustrated History of the 20th Century

"Women don't want their men to be boys; they want them to be men."
— Eileen Ford

"Beautiful men are not necessarily memorable-looking."
— Michelangelo Signorile

"I would never want to be with a guy whose jean size was smaller than mine or who took longer to do his hair than me."
— Cindy Crawford

"Heartthrob — isn't that an awful word?!"
— Tab Hunter

bibliography